THE MAN FROM DEVIL'S ISLAND

The Man From Devil's Island

COLIN RICKARDS

STEIN AND DAY/*Publishers*/New York

Library of Congress Catalog Card No. 68-17315

Printed in the United States of America
Stein and Day/*Publishers*/7 East 48 Street, New York, N.Y. 10017

For

M

who put up with a lot

ACKNOWLEDGEMENTS

The following publishers have generously permitted me to quote from books they have published and I take pleasure in acknowledging my debt to them: The Hutchinson Group for permission to quote from *Scars Are My Passport* by George John Seaton (1951); Max Parrish and Co. Ltd. for permission to use passages from *The Conquest of Devil's Island*, by Charles Pean (1953); E. P. Dutton and Co. Ltd., of New York, for permission to quote from *Dry Guillotine* (1938), and *Hell on Trial* (1940), both by René Belbenoit; and Cassells and Co. Ltd. for permission to quote from *Damned and Damned Again* by William Willis (1959). And a special note of thanks to Mrs. Merle Serano who laboured over the untidy first draft and turned it into a presentable manuscript.

INTRODUCTION

IN THE SUMMER of 1956 I was sitting in the sun outside a Parisian pavement-side café, up on the hill near Montmartre, planning my day's sightseeing. I was looking at a street guide when a ragged, bearded man stopped and asked for a light for a battered Gaulois cigarette.

The following day I was sitting at the same table when the man walked up. This time he dropped quietly into a chair and asked if I would buy him a coffee. Reluctantly, I agreed. It seemed easier than telling him to go away and might save me from a torrent of abuse.

Over the coffee I had a chance to study him. He looked very old—it turned out later that he was just under sixty. His lean face was deeply lined and his skin was burned to a dark mahogany colour. He could have been an Algerian—that had been my first thought—but on closer inspection I realised that he was obviously a European who had spent a lifetime in the tropics.

When I mentioned the sunburn he smiled thinly. Most of his teeth were gone and it was not a pleasant smile.

'*Le bagne*, monsieur,' he said.

And then the penny dropped. *Le bagne:* the slang name for the penal settlements of French Guiana, notorious throughout the world as Devil's Island.

I was instantly interested. I had read of the penal settlements from time to time. I had also read the books by the convict author René Belbenoit who escaped and found in America the sanctuary he needed to write shocking exposés of the prison camps.

My coffee-drinking companion told me that his name was Etienne Artaud. I did not—and still do not—believe him. But then what was more natural than for a man with a past like his to change his name? He had been sent to *le bagne* for killing his common-law wife—sent there for ten years to pay his debt to society.

His conversation was full of slang. He spoke with the modicum of words, sometimes lapsing into long periods of silence as though dredging up an almost-forgotten memory to answer some question I had asked. I repeatedly had to get him to explain the phrases and words he used.

I was hearing for the first time the tongue of *les durs*—convict slang for the penal colony. Phrases like *la guillotine sêche*—the dry guillotine as Victor Hugo had called French Guiana; *les condamnés*—the class of convicts made up of killers, rapists and blackmailers; and *mômes*—homosexual convicts—crept into the conversation and needed explanation.

Etienne Artaud told me a great deal on successive meetings. He had seen things that few men have survived to tell about. *Le bagne* killed off seven-eighths of the 80,000 men sent to Guiana between 1852 and 1938. He was one of the lucky 10,000 who came out alive. He spoke of public guillotinings; of men tied to trees and left there for forty-eight hours in the burning tropical sun as the punishment for some trivial offence; of the dreaded 'bear pits' on the punishment island of St. Joseph where convicts huddled in tiny underground cells, their only light a few bars above their head which let in the blistering heat during the day and the damp chill of the night.

This was the land of death, where men, harnessed like beasts, toiled out their lives in the forests, or broke rocks which would never be used for road-building. This was France's twentieth-century penal establishment.

Today *le bagne* is no more. France is building a missile tracking station on Devil's Island. The former colony is a Department of Metropolitan France. Moves are afoot to turn it into a tourist resort. But the ghosts of the 70,000 men who lived, fought and died like animals still haunt the place.

Occasionally over long periods of years rumblings came from the forgotten corner of the French Empire. Word would come out of Guiana with travellers, clergymen and lawyers and the outside world would hear of the horrors that were *le bagne*.

French Guiana, and more particularly Devil's Island, received a great deal of publicity in the last few years of the nineteenth century over the case of Alfred Dreyfus, the French army officer sent to *le bagne* for betraying secrets to an enemy power and eventually proven to have been wrongly convicted. France's most famous writers had come to Dreyfus's aid with pamphlets, articles and books about him, about the case, and about French Guiana. Men like Emile Zola, Anatole France and Joseph Reinach[1] all spoke up for Dreyfus.

The penal settlements in France's oldest colony had been world headline news and few people were unaware of their existence. Then, in the early years of the present century, came a disturbing report by the Protestant Pastor Paul Richard who had done mission work among the convicts from June, 1904, to January, 1905. Almost immediately this was followed by a tragic book by the anarchist Liard-Courtois who was on Devil's Island at the same time as Dreyfus.

The French public conscience got another jolt in 1925 from a series of articles by one of the country's most famous journalists and writers, Albert Londres. Six years later came a series of scorching articles by newspaperman Luc Dornain who had crossed the Atlantic on the prison ship *La Martinière* as a stowaway to see how the convicts were treated. The following year another series of articles shocked France. These, written by convict René Belbenoit at the instigation of a former prison governor in Guiana named Siadous, were appearing in the nationally distributed *Police Gazette* at a time when Belbenoit was in a French prison waiting to make his second journey to *le bagne*.

Years later Belbenoit, then an escaped convict, was in the United States. He wrote his story[2] which ran into several editions.

[1] *Histoire de l'Affaire Dreyfus* by Joseph Reinach (seven volumes published in Paris between 1901 and 1911).

[2] *Dry Guillotine* by René Belbenoit (E. P. Dutton, New York, 1938).

Warner Brothers filmed it and Belbenoit followed with another best-seller.[1]

As far as possible I have checked out Etienne Artaud's story against the records left by other convicts and by impartial observers. I have gathered figures to back up his statements from official reports and documents. In British Guiana[2] I talked with a retired Dutch colonial policeman whose job at one period was to prevent the convicts escaping across the Maroni River into Dutch Guiana.[3]

In police records and other official documents, and from personal contact with several escaped convicts in various parts of the Caribbean and Central America, I have pieced together the last two chapters which round off Etienne Artaud's story and also the chapter dealing with the various British subjects who were sent to the Guiana penal settlements.

About 900 men were sent to the settlements every year from the turn of the century. But there were never more than 6,000 convicts alive in the colony at any one time.

This book, then, is primarily the story of Etienne Artaud's twenty-one years in the living hell of the penal settlements that the world wrongly knows as Devil's Island. But it is also the story of the settlements themselves, the most notorious penal colony in the history of twentieth-century judicial correction.

COLIN RICKARDS

London, 1968

[1] *Hell on Trial* by René Belbenoit (E. P. Dutton, New York, 1940).

[2] Now independent as Guyana, but the name by which it was known at the time of the story will be used throughout the book.

[3] Now called Surinam and a part in its own right of the Kingdom of the Netherlands.

THE MAN FROM DEVIL'S ISLAND

CHAPTER ONE

IT WAS RAINING when I left work, the sort of cold, damp rain which soaks you to the skin and chills you to the bone. The sky was dark and heavy and it looked as if the evening would be even worse than the afternoon. I was going home earlier than usual because the manager was in a good mood and had told us to down tools.

I had promised Marie that I would take her out in the evening, but I knew that if the rain kept on she would not want to go. It suited me well enough. I walked down our street and pushed my key into the front door lock. She was not downstairs and I thought that she must be out shopping.

Leaving my wet shoes in the hall I went upstairs to change my clothes. As I reached the landing I heard voices. One of them belonged to Marie. The other voice was a stranger to me. It belonged to a man. The door of our bedroom was slightly open and I paused listening, feeling slightly guilty as I did so.

As I stood there I heard Marie's giggle and then the rhythmic creaking of the bed springs. I took a quick step across the landing and flung open the door.

Marie was naked on the bed, her long legs wrapped around the man on top of her. As the door slammed back she twisted her mouth away from his and looked towards me. Her grey eyes became wide and her mouth opened in a scream. It came as I leapt into the room and grabbed a brass poker from where it stood in the hearth.

The man never had a chance. He was only half off the bed when the poker caught him across the side of the face and hurled him into a corner. I was after him in a second, leaping across the bed in my stockinged feet and smashing the poker down on his head as he tried to get up. I kept hitting him until he lay still, his skull fractured and bloody.

Then, and only then, did I become fully aware of Marie's screaming. She was lying face down on the bed, her hands twisting the pillow under her and screaming at the top of her voice. I brought the poker down on the back of her head and she stopped suddenly.

Once the room was quiet again I became calm. I looked at the poker in my hands and the two naked and bloody bodies. And then I heard the banging on the door. I went down the stairs and let in the policeman who had been summoned by neighbours alerted by Marie's screams.

That was all there was to it.

I was tried at Pau Assizes and my lawyer did everything that he could for me. The judge ruled out the clause in the law that allowed a man to protect the sanctity of his home, and which normally would have condoned my actions.

Technically ours was not a 'home'. For, though Marie and I had lived together for four gloriously happy years, we were not married. And the law recognised only a legal alliance as constituting a 'home'. Added to that, I had not only killed the man involved, I had killed Marie as well.

I have no complaint against the judge. He acted fairly according to the law. It was my misfortune. He was a humane man, however, and while he could have sent me to the guillotine for murder he did not do so.

Instead he sentenced me to ten years at hard labour in the penal settlements of French Guiana. It probably seemed a very reasonable sentence to him.

But, then, he did not know *le bagne*.

I was twenty-four years old in June, 1924. He probably felt that when I returned to France I would still be a young man and would be able to reshape my life.

I was allowed to receive books during the time that I was waiting to be transferred to St. Martin-de-Ré, where convicts were held to await the ship which took them to Guiana. My lawyer spent hours discussing *le bagne* with me and explaining the various kinds of prisoners who were sent there. In the books I read I learned some of the history of the place in which I was to spend the next ten years of my life.

The convict settlements in French Guiana, scattered like festering sores across the face of France's only possession in South America, were established to colonise an outpost of empire. Instead, they became a living death for every man sent there; a dismal failure as a colony—for much of it to this day is still neither explored nor settled; and the most notorious penal settlement in the world.

Geographically, French Guiana lies between 1° 30′ and 5° 50′ north and 51° 40′ and 54° 30′ west. To the north is the Atlantic Ocean; to the south are the grim and forbidding Tumac Humac Mountains and on the far side of them, Brazil; the western neighbour is Dutch Guiana with the Maroni River as the border; the eastern neighbour is Brazil, with the Oyapock River as the border. From the coast to the Tumac Humac is 250 miles of dense snake-infested jungle. The coastline is two hundred miles long. The country, now a Department of Metropolitan France, but once their oldest colony, covers 35,135 square miles on the north coast of South America.

The first Frenchmen reached Guiana in 1604 under the explorer and adventurer Daniel de La Ravadière who was seeking Eldorado, the mythical city of the Incas. He landed at Cayenne, failed to find the golden empire and sailed for home. Several mercantile companies tried to settle colonists at Cayenne without much success during the next fifty years and in 1686, an expedition under the privateer Jean Baptiste Ducasse was decimated by the military in Dutch Guiana.

It put an end to French rule for the next fifteen years, but between 1700 and 1763 the family of Orvilliers held the nominal governorship of the colony. France's then Prime Minister, the Duc de Choiseul, tried to settle colonists at Kourou, midway along the coastline, in 1763 but they fell prey to fever, his 14,000 colonists died like flies, only 3,000 of them surviving the first two years. But the tenacious few held on and by 1788 it was estimated that there were 1,300 whites, 400 free Negroes and 10,500 slaves living in the colony. The French Revolution brought emancipation and many slaves ran away and established themselves in the jungle, going back to their African tribal life. They are there to this day, known as Bush Negroes—tiny portions of West Africa preserved in the New World.

Consul Victor Hugues, who was active throughout France's possessions in the Caribbean, re-established slavery and an Anglo-Portuguese expedition took Guiana away from the French in 1809. The colony was restored eight years later and prospered once more under French rule. Between 1827 and 1846 Mother Anne Marie Javouhey, superior of St. Joseph of Cluny, a mission founded at Mana, established a prosperous centre of free Negroes. Complete emancipation came in 1848 and with it came the decay of the sugar and logwood empires. The French tried to replace the Negro labourers with several thousand Hindus from India as indentured workers and then by other labour from the French possessions in Indo-China. But they soon discovered that when their period of indentured time was worked out the Asians either opened shops or set up on their own smallholdings. Everywhere sugar cane rotted for want of men to harvest it. Big plantations which had made absentee French owners fabulously wealthy tumbled into decay and the price of land fell. At one time it was almost impossible to give away a plantation.

And then, midway through the century, Louis Napoleon thought he had found the answer.

Did slaves, or virtual slaves, have to be black or brown? he asked himself. Why not use white convict labour where coloured forced labour had been used? And at the same time why not rid France for ever of the costs of maintaining prisons for convicts who would never be reformed and merely continue to prey on the public?

Accordingly, the first shipment of convicts left France for Guiana on 27 March, 1852. They were 354 of the worst men in the country's prisons: murderers, rapists, violent criminals, political prisoners, incorrigible thieves. They arrived at Cayenne on 12 May and thus began what was to become a regular traffic for the next eighty-six years.

For most of the convicts it was a one-way ticket to hell.

In the first year a total of 2,220 convicts were shipped from France and by 1867 about 18,000 men had been sent to French Guiana 'to start a new life in a new land for the glory of France', as the official designation for Transportation put it at the time.

But the sugar plantations were too far gone to be reclaimed by the unwilling work of the convict labourers. Instead they were put into camps to cut wood, break rocks and toil in the tropical sun until their sentences expired—or they did.

They died: of leprosy; of malnutrition; of tropical fevers; of anaemia. They were beaten to death by warders; shot trying to escape; worked in fever-ridden settlements until they dropped. They killed each other for shirts; for a few centimes; for real and imagined grievances; and sometimes for fun. They died of broken hearts; of worms; of syphilis; and because there was nothing better to do.

The original Articles of Transportation were designed to include every man sentenced to more than five years' imprisonment, and they were soon expanded to give a system under which certain classes of criminals might regain their right to live in France. In theory it was fine. In practice it seldom worked. Few men lived long enough to complete their sentences.

I learned that the convicts were divided into three grades: *déportés*, *transportés* and *relégués*, and that these last two could be again subdivided. *Transportés* were men sentenced to penal servitude for murder, rape, sexual crimes, robbery with violence or other major offences. Most worked in the forced labour camps but a few, the *assignés*, were employed by private individuals in the colony which paid the French Government fifty francs a month for each man. Ten francs were returned to the *assigné*, making this a cheap form of indentured labour. *Concessionnaires* were of two kinds: some were allocated a small piece of ground which they worked and lived off, this being the nearest thing to the proposed colonisation that ever took place in French Guiana; other *concessionnaires* worked for the Government or for private individuals in lumber camps, in workshops or on farms.

The *transporté* was free to return to France after he had completed both his sentence and a period known as *doublage*, which was the same length as the original sentence. Thus, a man sent to Guiana for ten years—as I was—served ten years as a convict and then another ten years as a free man—a *libéré* he was called—before he was allowed to return home.

Déportés were men who, under a law dated 8 June, 1850, were sent to Guiana as political prisoners, enemies of the state, traitors, seditious pamphleteers and spies. They began their sentences on Devil's Island, a tiny rock off the mainland, where they lived without guards, and with only the sharks and the pounding surf as their gaolers. After fifteen years they might be transferred to the mainland settlements. They, too, were free to return to France after completion of their sentences and *doublage*—but most were sentenced to life.

Relégués, technically, were the cream of the colony. They were incorrigibles who had been in and out of French gaols for petty crimes—larceny, vagrancy and minor theft. Under a law passed in May, 1885, *Relégation* was defined as 'life imprisonment in colonial territory'.

To quote from Article Four: 'Men who will be classed as *relégués*: old offenders who during a period of ten years—not inclusive of periods of detention—have received (i) Two sentences of penal servitude or solitary confinement, (ii) A sentence to penal servitude or solitary confinement plus two sentences for robbery, (iii) Three sentences of more than three months, (iv) Seven sentences of which two at least were of more than three months.'

The *relégués* were supposed to work as virtual free men building up the economy and resources of the colony. They were, in fact, the worst-off of all the men sent to Guiana.

The status set-up of convicts in Guiana was further complicated by the fact that men might commit crimes while in the colony which would change their lives completely.

A *relégué* who was found guilty of a serious crime in the Settlements would be punished. But the punishment itself was ambiguous. As a *relégué* he could never return to France. But being punished for a very serious crime made him a *transporté* by definition. All that it meant at the time of the punishment was that the man was transferred from the *relégué* camp at St. Jean to the *transporté* camp at St. Laurent.[1]

By the same token a *transporté* who was a *libéré*—doing his *doublage* preparatory to being sent back to France—might well be arrested several times for vagrancy and having no means of support in one of the coastal towns. Under the 1852 law which defined *relégués* he would then be reclassified. Thus he would become classed as a *relégué*, be sent to a work camp and be prevented for ever from returning home.

As the Salvation Army officer in Guiana once put it: 'The various sections of the Settlements thus exchanged their miserable clients and there were very few who contrived to escape the meshes of this net.'

Everything was weighted heavily against the convict.

Doublage—conceived originally to provide the convict with a period of readjustment during which it was hoped he would settle down and not want to return to France—turned out to be one of the most infamous aspects of French Guiana. In fact it was extremely successful in preventing men from returning to France. Most of them were dead long before this 'second sentence' was completed. Napoleon III had had the idea that the men would marry the local women in the colony and raise children. Then, their *doublage* completed, they would be unwilling to pull up all ties, leave their families and return to France. But few of the Guianese women would have anything to do with the shambling wrecks of humanity who were these

[1] At the beginning of 1927 there were 2,193 *relégués* on the rosters of *le bagne*. By the end of the year 178 had died and 402 had escaped—*Conquest of Devil's Island* by Captain Charles Pean.

libérés.[1] And, should a man manage to exist long enough to complete his *doublage*, it was unlikely that he would have enough money—or have relatives still in touch with him who could send the money—for the passage home. *Doublage* was finally abolished in 1940.

In the first fifteen years of the convict settlement's existence France sent 18,000 men to French Guiana.

One of the first to arrive, as well as to escape and make newspaper headlines, was the burglar Poncet who was sent to Guiana in 1855. Within a year he and a companion had escaped into the jungle hoping to hide out until the search for them was abandoned. Days later Poncet's companion died and the burglar risked returning to Cayenne under cover of darkness. As dawn was breaking he saw a ship in the harbour preparing to sail and tried to get aboard as a stowaway.

But the town was full of guards and by the time Poncet reached the dock the ship was under sail. Desperately oblivious of sharks, he jumped into the sea and began swimming. Six hours later the ship lay becalmed and Poncet swam alongside. He was picked up and taken to the United States.

Then began a remarkable story.

He fought for the Union in the American Civil War and then emigrated to England and lived for some years in Liverpool. There he met a wealthy Frenchman who employed him as a valet. When he was returning to France his employer bought forged papers for Poncet and they returned together. Back in France the former burglar repaid his benefactor's kindness by slitting his throat for his wallet—a crime for which he quite properly went to the guillotine.

More men were awaiting shipment to *le bagne* in 1888 when there was a change in penal policy and it was decided to colonise and populate the French island of New Caledonia in the South

[1] In 1927 there were 2,393 *libérés* in the penal colony; 319 were at Cayenne, 600 in St. Laurent and the others were scattered about the various coastal settlements of Mana, Sinamary and l'Aprouaque—*Conquest of Devil's Island* by Captain Charles Pean.

Seas. Convicts sent there received grants of land at the expiration of their sentences. But the experiment lasted for only a few years and then Guiana became once more the main penal colony.

Each of the three tiny islands off the coast—Royale, St. Joseph and Devil's Island—had its own formidable story to tell.

Originally they had been settled—and named—by the survivors of the 14,000 colonists sent out by the Duc de Choiseul. After thousands had died on the mainland the rest, led by Chevalier Turgot, put to sea in open boats and headed for the three islands. There was no malaria there and the fresh sea breezes kept the mosquitoes, sandflies and other insect pests from reaching them.

Les Isles du Salut—the Isles of Salvation—the colonists called them. Isle Royale they named in honour of the king; St. Joseph after the saint under whose divine protection they had sailed; the third, nearest to the mainland, they called Isle du Diable—Devil's Island—because the turbulence of the sea in the narrow channel between it and Isle Royale convinced Turgot that the devil lived there.

They continued to live on Isle Royale until time and the tropics took their toll.

Devil's Island, only nine miles from the mainland, was reserved for political prisoners. Probably the best-known prisoner in the history of French Guiana was Alfred Dreyfus, the Army officer who was sent to Devil's Island as a traitor but who was innocent of the charge. It is because 'Devil's Island' has a romantic ring to it that to the outside world the whole penal colony became known by that name.

The other two islands later became places of punishment for the penal colony.

This was Guiana—*le bagne*—where I was to spend ten years—if I survived.

CHAPTER TWO

Convicts due for transportation to *le bagne* were assembled at Ile de Ré, a tiny island in the Bay of Biscay. I was taken there in chains to join men from every major prison in France: from Santé, the dreaded prison of Paris; from La Rochelle; from Riom, where the discipline was the most severe; from Marseilles and Brest and Toulon. We were murderers, traitors, sex perverts, petty thieves. Convicts all; destination Guiana.

We crossed by a ferry and marched to the prison, a grim moated fortress, built by Vauban as a defence against the English. It had only one entrance or exit, across a drawbridge and under a grey stone arch. Senegalese soldiers guarded the archway with its effigies of Louis XIV. Our clothing, issued at previous prisons, was taken from us and in its place we received a red and white striped shirt, a pair of coarse brown trousers, a pair of wooden clogs, a cap, a blanket and a kit bag. We were given an ice-cold shower, whipped by guards for not getting into the water quickly and whipped again for not getting dry soon enough. Next we went to the barber who shaved our heads. And then we were taken to the cells.

That first night we were chained together—not for any misdemeanour, but, as the warden explained, as a warning against any trouble that we might make, while awaiting shipment.

I and the men with me had just missed a sailing for *le bagne* and we were told that we would have to wait at St. Martin-de-Ré for six or eight months. They were the winter months and that was our misfortune. The cells were old, stone, damp and cold. If a convict caught pneumonia it was just too bad. Either he recovered—or there was one less passenger for *le bagne*.

The convict ship *La Martinière* was owned by the French Line who hired her out to the French Government when enough convicts had been collected at St. Martin-de-Ré to make a trip to Guiana worth while. Originally she was owned by a British Company and was built at West Hartlepool in 1911. She weighed 3,718 tons and was bought by the French Line, especially for convict carrying, to replace *La Loire* which was sunk in mid-Atlantic in 1916 by German action during the First World War.

A man named Rousseau joined us after we had been at St. Martin for about three months. He was a killer who had escaped from *le bagne* in 1921 after serving three years of a life sentence. He had reached Venezuela, taken a ship to Spain and then crossed into France, thinking that he could live there undetected. He had had two years of freedom and then, by one of those odd chances of life, met a former schoolmate on the street. The man was a gendarme and arrested Rousseau at once.

We who were awaiting shipment to *le bagne* pumped him full of questions about the place—and mostly about the chances of escape. We all hoped that Guiana was going to be a jungle paradise where escape—*la belle*, Rousseau called it—would be easy. He soon shattered our illusions.

He wetted his finger and traced a map of Guiana on the stone floor of the cell. Then he began to tell us why escape was so difficult.

There were four directions a convict could take when leaving *le bagne*: the four points of the compass. Each had obstacles which only a superman—or a man driven by extraordinary forces—could overcome. To the east was bush, swamps and jungle—Brazil; to the west lay Dutch Guiana, across the wide and treacherous Maroni River, then more bush, more jungle; to the south, 250 miles away through parts of French Guiana even today unexplored and inhabited by savage Indians, were the Tumac Humac Mountains and beyond them the Amazon basin; to the north, seven hundred miles away, across shark-infested seas, were the islands of the Caribbean.

Everything was stacked against the escaper.

The jungle was dense and treacherous and many of the Indian tribes and some of the Bush Negroes would turn in an escaping convict for the price the French put on his head. The Saramaca headhunters were particularly to be feared. So were the cannibal Indians. They received one hundred francs for a convict's head—and no questions asked about what happened to the rest of him.

The smugglers from Brazil who occasionally put into St. Laurent were not to be trusted, Rousseau said. They demanded a thousand francs to smuggle a convict aboard and then as soon as they were off their own coast he was likely to be murdered, robbed of anything of value and thrown overboard.

The Chinese traders at St. Laurent supplemented their incomes by selling canoes to convicts planning to escape across the Maroni to Dutch Guiana or to try their luck on the run to Trinidad. The Bush Negroes who visited the town to sell produce and buy coffee, knives and trinkets also sold boats—usually dugouts burned out of tree trunks—to would-be escapers.

He told a story about one of the local Guianese, a man named Bichier des Ages, who had established himself in a racket which worked well for a long time.

For a set fee Bichier sold escapes. He supplied a canoe to take the men across the Maroni and food, medical supplies, bush knives and even a gun for the assault on the jungle on the other side. The would-be escaper just paid the all-inclusive fee and then met Bichier at the appointed hour and place. His reputation among the convicts was high. Not one of the many escaping convicts who had done business with him had ever been returned to the Settlements. He was the most famous seller of escapes in St. Laurent. He even had a waiting list of clients.

And then one day an Arab convict came stumbling out of the jungle more dead than alive. He had a bullet in his shoulder and a fantastic story to tell. By night-fall every convict in St. Laurent knew it.

Bichier des Ages, escape-seller supreme, had evolved a plan. He would guide the escapers to a secluded spot in the jungle where the boat was supposed to be, shoot them down and then rob and bury them.

That was why none of his clients had ever been returned to *le bagne*.

A week later he was a convict himself, Rousseau said with satisfaction.

It did not sound at all hopeful, but we consoled ourselves with the thought that Rousseau had escaped. If he could do it, so could we. And we would not get caught as he had been.

Rousseau also taught us the unique lingo of *le bagne*. The convicts had coined their own language and lived by just one rule—survival of the fittest.

Le bagne, les durs, la guillotine sêche—The Dry Guillotine—were all names they gave to the penal colony itself. They called the mainland settlements *Grand Terre*. A convict was a *forçat*. A warder was a *gaffe*. Escape was *la belle*. The toughest convicts, usually the murderers or former big-time gangsters, ruled the others by force and often made them do their work under threats of violence. These men was called *fort-à-bras*—strong-arm men. A *mouchard* was a stool-pigeon, a nark, an informer. An *inco* was a convict who was an incorrigible trouble-maker or escaper. A *condamné* was a convict; a *prévôt*, a trusty. *Evasion* was an escape or an attempted escape. An *évadé* was the escaper. *Tafia* was the raw bush rum that was made by the Indians or Bush Negroes. A *stère* was the amount of wood that men in the forced labour camps were expected to cut each day. It is a cubic metre of wood —about thirty-six cubic feet.

Finally there was the *plan* which every man carried. The convicts, whatever their official status, were prohibited from owning anything other than what was issued to them by the Administration—a blanket and a few clothes. They were specifically forbidden to have any money, other than the pittance that was officially paid to them, for sums of ready cash might enable a man to buy a canoe and make an escape. They were frequently searched and so evolved the idea of a *plan*. This was a hollow tube of metal—preferably aluminium or steel—which screwed apart. Inside it banknotes could be hidden. So could a few jewels if the man was fortunate enough to have any. The *plan* was then secreted in the anal cavity, the only place where a naked man could possibly hide anything. Coins, which would not fit into the *plan*, were generally swallowed time after time until they came to be spent.

After five months in the cold dungeons of St. Martin-de-Ré the warden came one morning and told us that we would be leaving for Guiana. *La Martinière*, the prison ship, had arrived.

At dawn two days later we were herded out of our cells and marched along corridors to the bathhouse. After that we lined up for an inoculation against typhus before being sent up into the main courtyard. Senegalese soldiers, their faces black as ebony and heads topped with red fezzes, stood about with rifles and fixed bayonets while we were lined up for the march to the landing docks and the barges which would take us out to the ship.

The hold of *La Martinière* was divided into eight sections, four to starboard and four to port. In each one was a cage, measuring some sixty feet long by twelve feet wide and twelve feet high, which became the home for eighty or ninety men on the voyage. Hammocks—enough for about half the men—hung from the ceiling. Those who did not get hammocks, usually the weak who could not fight for them, slept on the floor in the spew and filth from the latrine bucket that stood in the corner and slopped or tipped over when the ship rolled.

I was one of the lucky ones who got a hammock. It was right next to the one which Rousseau took. He knew the ropes and I had decided to watch what he did and make sure that I followed suit.

He warned me that discipline was harsh. The slightest sound of a minor scuffle and the guards would rush in and rain blows on everyone within reach. A serious insurrection could be instantly crushed by one guard who, turning a stop valve, could send steam from the boilers straight into the cage through the open-ended pipes which ran along the ceiling above our hammocks.

Rousseau told me about his crime and I told him what I had

done. A lot of the other men in the cage claimed to have been wrongly convicted and Rousseau laughed. Perhaps one out of the eighty-three of us might be innocent, he said.

And he told us a story that had taken place a few months before he escaped from *le bagne*. It was about Jean Guien, who was convicted in 1906 of murdering an English showgirl called Muriel Hayes. At first Guien had been condemned to death. Then a reprieve came and he was sent to Guiana for life. He did not manage to escape from *le bagne* until 1921. But after he escaped, a man in the hands of the Paris police signed a confession that he had killed Muriel Hayes sixteen years before.

The Ministry of Justice ordered Guien to be returned to France but the Administration could not find him. He had been written off as an *évadé*, having escaped into the jungle three months before. Nearly five months later guards on the trail of another fugitive stumbled across Guien living in a hut in the backwoods swamps. He was alive but quite mad. He was desperately weak from fever and malnutrition when they took him back to the camp. A few hours before he died a doctor told him that his name had been cleared.

Rousseau liked the story because he felt that it proved two points: that few men were sent to Guiana without cause—but that it could happen; and that it was almost impossible to escape, as he had told us.

The other convicts thought of him as a *fort-à-bras*, so nobody troubled him and because I had become his friend they did not try to trouble me either.

It soon became obvious who the *fort-à-bras* in our cage would be. They were hardened criminals, most of them, and had somehow managed to bring knives on board. They fought each other for supremacy, but even the most ferocious fight was usually carried out in complete silence. Nobody wanted the guards to rush in and beat everyone within reach; or, worse still, the steam to be turned on.

There were also other punishments on *La Martinière*.

Particularly difficult convicts were taken from their cages and put in the special 'hot room', a tiny airless hole next to the boilers, from which they emerged scarlet and blistered from the intense heat. Another disciplinary device was the 'Bench of Justice', a narrow ledge about five feet from the ground. A man would be forced to sit on the ledge—a scant three inches wide—with his back to the bars and his hands pushed through them and manacled behind him so that he could not fall off. After a few hours on this seat a man would be crippled for weeks afterwards with torn and strained muscles. Convicts who were to be clapped in irons had their bare feet thrust through the bars of the cage and manacled together so that they could not draw them back or stand up. They just had to lie there in the spew and the contents of the latrine bucket that swirled about them like a putrid sea.

The food was terrible. At meal times we were broken up into groups of about twenty and two men from each group were taken under guard to carry iron pans from the galley. What passed for stew was ladled on to shallow tin plates and we ate it with a spoon. In fact that was all we required. There was nothing that could be cut and little that was big enough to have needed a fork. When the food was spilled by the carriers it could not be replaced and several times, when the sea was particularly rough, the day's ration was lost. However, as practically everyone was being seasick at the time, it hardly mattered. The spew added to the contents of the latrine bucket and those who had no hammocks either bunked in with mates or stayed in the swill which filled the bottom of the cage.

Twice a day we were 'washed', a simple operation as the sailors stuck sea hoses through the bars of the cages and hosed us down. For one hour each day we were taken up on to the deck for 'exercise' and made to stand in rows facing the sea. Talking was forbidden. If a man spoke he was dragged away and whipped. Even when the ship entered the tropics we were forced to stand in the burning sun and many of the men fainted. They were just left where they lay.

It took between fourteen and twenty-three days to make the trip from France to French Guiana. We were lucky, it took us only fifteen days. Men must have been half-crazed on a longer crossing.

One morning the guard in charge of our cell seemed in a better mood than usual and at lunchtime he told us that we had arrived off Guiana. We were keen for the exercise period and stood along the rails watching the shore, palm fringed and sandy, giving way to blue-green massed foliage further inland.

Here it was; land of escape; tropical paradise.

Or so we told ourselves.

CHAPTER THREE

THE MARCH TO the Camp de la Transportation gave us an inkling of what life might be like. *Libérés*, their lustreless eyes in sallow, emaciated faces, watched us from their hovels as we were double-marched from the docks. The guards barked commands and swished their whips at us so that we would not dawdle. We could see the dark brown Maroni River swirling slowly to the sea. Albina, the Dutch frontier settlement directly across the river, was a bunch of tiny white houses shimmering in the tropical heat haze that hung over the country, distorting everything more than half a mile away. The jungle was a solid mass of intense colour, almost blue in the merciless sun.

We reached the dark wooden gates of the Camp de la Transportation and halted before the white cement arch, *La Porte Noire*—the Black Gate—they called it. And 'The Gate of Hell'.

We stood there watching a gang of convicts who had been out on a work detail being checked in. They were terrible looking men wearing straw hats with wide brims darkened by the sun and rains. Their uniforms were not a solid red, but red and white striped. The stripes ran up and down and made it look as if blood ran down the bodies of the wearers. They shuffled rather than walked and their faces were grey, fleshless and oddly alike. They had been halted opposite us and the guards began to search them. Arab *prévôts*—trusties—frisked them with practised thoroughness, even taking off their straw hats so that they could not smuggle food in on their heads.

We followed them through the gate and saw them march away to huts inside the high wall. We were taken to another part of the camp and there divided into three groups according to our prison status: *transportés*, *deportés* or *relégués*. We would spend a week there, we were told, and would then be sent to different camps.

That night, shackled by the right ankle to our wooden beds, we listened to stories of *le bagne* from an old convict who had been put into our hut to brief us on life in the settlements.

He warned us not to anger the guards who were largely drawn from NCOs in the disciplinary battalions of the French Army, from the Foreign Legion, past masters of corrective discipline, and from the toughest and cruellest of the warders in France's prisons. Throughout their fifteen-year terms in Guiana they were almost as much prisoners as we were. We outnumbered them twenty to one and fear of a rebellion made them enforce the rules with ruthless efficiency. Boredom brought out their most sadistic streaks. The Corsicans, in particular, ruled Guiana with the whip and the boot, ordering the harshest punishments for the most trifling crimes. The only guards who ever showed any real degree of humanity were the dozen or so Negroes—from Guiana or the French West Indian islands. They were stern enforcers of the rules, but retained their dignity and did not indulge in the cold-blooded sadism of some of their white counterparts. We came to know that we would get a square deal from them.

Guards lived in huts in the official quarters, married prostitutes or carried on homosexual relationships with convicts. Those that were married had often drawn their wives from the dock-land brothels of Marseilles, Brest and Toulon. They notified the authorities that they wanted to get married and the waterfront whores in custody at the time were given a choice: prison or marriage to a warder in French Guiana. Most chose marriage. The guards were paid 150 francs a day—about 15s.—and served two years in Guiana before their first leave, a six-month passage-paid trip to France. There were three hundred of them scattered about the settlements and they were supplemented by an equal number of *prévôts*—trusties—most of them Arabs.

Our 'old timer' had been in *le bagne* for three years and knew the ropes. He was heavily tattooed and told us that it was a common practice. The following day we saw this for ourselves. Chests were ornamented with obscene phrases and pictures.

Napoleon in a cocked hat glared interminably at a lavatory wall with obscene messages on it. Snakes writhed down sinewy arms. Couples making love moved suggestively when the muscles on a back were flexed. 'Enfant de Malheur'—child of misfortune—was a popular phrase. A thick blue line round the neck mocking the guillotine would read 'Cut here and be damned'. More literary convicts might choose 'The past has cheated me, the present torments me, the future appals me'. Others had the date of their crimes tattooed on their chests. An art forger named François Lagrange was the best tattooist in *le bagne*.

We were warned against the *fort-à-bras* and Arab *prévôts* who were homosexuals almost to a man and were always on the lookout for young convicts among the new arrivals. They would bribe, cajole or beat them into becoming their 'little friends'—*mômes* in the language of *le bagne*.

We were at St. Laurent for a week and had ample opportunity to see this in action. Oddly, it did not happen in our hut, but convicts in other huts told us of vicious beatings and silent knife fights over young convicts by the self-appointed *fort-à-bras*. Some of the *mômes* enjoyed their new position. Some rebelled against it. They were gambled for over cards, sold to raise money for escapes, fought over, and defended against other *fort-à-bras* by their boy-friends. The guards were bribed to make life easier for the *mômes* who then took on all the sickening aspects of the long-time pansy, painting their lips, powdering their faces with chalk and plucking their eyebrows. If they tried to break away from their virtual owners they were beaten or worse.

One *môme* I knew of who thought to assert his masculinity and get a *môme* of his own, was dragged into the bush by his boy-friend—a *relégué* named Kleisser—and castrated to 'put an end to his crazy notions' as the master put it.

The boy-friends bought them cosmetics from the convicts who operated the little rail-cars that ran from St. Laurent to the inland camps and smuggled on the side, and kept them supplied with cigarettes, mirrors and sweets. Often they openly referred to them as their 'wives'.

1. A mass consignment of 673 convicts are marched to the prison ship which will take them to servitude in Guiana.—Associated Press Photo

2. Etienne Artaud (at right between French officer and Arab prisoner) and a group of fellow convicts being marched from the prison to the transport ship *La Martinière*.—Associated Press Photo

Many *mômes* tolerated their new-found status at first and eventually grew to enjoy it. They did not have to work as hard, their battles were fought for them, and their lot was comparatively easy compared with that of the majority of convicts. After lights out the *mômes* busied themselves at their mirrors, plucking their eyebrows, painting their lips and powdering their faces. If their boy-friends had been able to buy some perfume from the smugglers, they used that.

And, if their boy-friends escaped or were killed, they just passed on to the next man strong enough to compete with other prospective boy-friends for their favours.

Le bagne, it became clear to us during that first week, moved on graft. It oiled the machinery of the Administration. It supplemented the guards' pay. It made life easier for every *fort-à-bras* who bribed or fought his way into an official position. The only ones who suffered from it were the general run of *transportés* and *relégués*.

The most famous story of corruption in *le bagne* involved a large clock that was sent out to decorate the St. Laurent hospital building but which never reached its destination having been sold *en route*. It was erected on a church across the river in Albina, the frontier town of Dutch Guiana.

As prisoners we were not allowed to receive money from France. But there was a way round it. Incoming mail for all prisoners was censored and accompanying money was confiscated. Incoming mail for the guards was not touched. We soon learned that we could have money sent to a guard who would then take twenty-five or thirty per cent for his 'services' before handing the rest to us. The scheme worked well for both parties. This graft was one thing over which the guards were usually honest. If a guard once took all the money the word soon got around and no other convict would have money sent through him. But if he took only the normal 'commission' he stood a chance of accumulating a considerable sum of money over a period of time as the convicts would always use him as the contact man. Only when it became known that a guard had nearly completed his tour of service in *le bagne* did we consider him a danger, as he might keep the money and take it with him. He had nothing to lose.

The book-keepers of the settlements were usually *fort-à-bras* who had bribed their way into the position because it offered freedom from the back-breaking toil of the wood-chopping camps and gave them almost endless possibilities for graft.

We soon heard the story of Laston, a murderer from Marseilles, who had killed at least four other men in Guiana and was the book-keeper at the *relégué* camp of St. Jean for many years. He was also one of the wealthiest men in the Settlements.

If a guard put a man on a charge Laston would forget to enter it on the sheet for a hundred francs. If a man wanted to get a transfer from a bush camp to an easier camp, he saw Laston and it could be arranged if he had the money. If a man wanted to go into the town of St. Laurent to buy *tafia*—the local bush rum—he saw Laston and his name disappeared from the daily duty role for a few days. If a *fort-à-bras* wanted to go into the jungle to trade with the Indians or cross the Maroni to steal from the Dutch, he would see Laston and his name would disappear from the duty rosters. His *môme* also was excused duties so that he could look after the *fort-à-bras*' belongings.

Laston and a guard had a racket selling clothing and blankets meant for the convicts to the local Guianese. Men who were due to draw new equipment often turned up to find that Laston had made a false entry in a ledger showing that they had had equipment a few weeks before. There was no use arguing.

A guard ran a little shop on each camp and the convicts could buy soap, toothpaste, paper and tobacco. Most of it was stolen from the Administration stores.

The camp cooks traded in food. In partnership with a trusty whose job it was to see that food was not stolen from the cook-house, he would make up parcels of food for convicts who paid for it. Some wanted it for escapes, some because they were perpetually hungry. Twice a week were 'meat days'. But the general run of us seldom saw much of it. The guard in charge took a share, the cook took a share, the kitchen trusty took a share, and so did his friends. When the meat got to us it was little more than fat and gristle.

Every official and minor official in *le bagne* had his own particular line of graft and they all grew rich. And while they did so men starved to death for the want of food.

For years Laston carried on an affair with the wife of one of the guards, but eventually he got over-confident and the husband come home to find Laston in bed with the wife. He gave Laston a whipping and then charged him with attempted rape. He was sent to St. Laurent for trial and given five years on St. Joseph. He ended up in the lunatic asylum after a few months. The guard beat up his wife so badly that she was in hospital for several weeks and was marked for life.

CHAPTER FOUR

AFTER A WEEK at the Camp de la Transportation I was assigned to work on Colonial Highway Number One. This was the official name for what we convicts called 'The Road to Nowhere' or 'Route Zero'.

In the 1880s it had been decided to build a road from St. Laurent to Cayenne, a distance of 160 miles through impenetrable jungle and bottomless swamps. The graft which moved *le bagne* swung into action at once. Machinery sent from France to be used in building the road was promptly sold to Dutch agriculturalists and planters across the Maroni and the wretched *transportés* were made to build the road, virtually with their bare hands.

I was put into a camp about twenty miles from St. Laurent which at that time was the furthest extent of 'The Road to Nowhere'. I worked on the road for six months. All around me men died in their hundreds. Men who had been my friends on the ship coming over just gave up. They hanged themselves from the liana vines. They slashed their wrists with axes. We fought among ourselves when we had hardly the strength to lift the axes. Once I sank in a swamp up to my neck and I would have drowned then and there if two friends had not pulled me out.

We used to say that 'Route Zero' had been thought up just to kill off convicts.

In fifty years only twenty-four miles of road were built. It is still there, or as much of it as the jungle has not taken back as its own. It winds into the bush eastward from St. Laurent—literally a 'Road to Nowhere'. Every yard marks the place where a man or several men died. These fifty years and twenty-four miles took the lives of ten thousand convicts before Colonial Highway Number One was officially abandoned.

One of the men on my work gang was a *fort-à-bras* named Schwartz who had been sent to *le bagne* for ten years for assaulting a little girl whose body he had then cut up and buried in a public park in Metz. He had tried one of the most audacious escape plans I ever heard of and very nearly got away with it.

Schwartz had come out as a *transporté* but after two years in Guiana he had beaten up a warder and been sentenced to three extra years at the punishment camp at Kourou, followed by relegation, which meant that he was bound to Guiana for life. They put him to work on 'Route Zero' thinking that it would kill him off. But when I arrived there he was in his fourth month, the only man there who was in any kind of physical condition bordering on the normal. I soon learned that this was because he took for himself part of the food ration of every convict in his work gang. If we complained he beat us—and the guards sometimes joined in as well. So we got by on two-thirds rations and hoped that a snake would get Schwartz.

A month later he was sent back to the *relégué* camp at St. Jean and we breathed a sigh of relief. Several years later I learned what had happened to him.

At St. Jean he began an illicit affair with the wife of the head warder, a man named Goulin, and the two of them evolved an escape plan with ingenuity born of desperation.

Goulin was due to be sent back to France at the end of his tour of duty. But his wife and Schwartz had other ideas. Goulin's papers, ticket and passport were waiting for him at St. Laurent. The baggage had been sent on ahead. Mme. Goulin arranged with a civilian photographer in St. Laurent to substitute Goulin's passport picture for one of Schwartz. Her plan was to go to the Administration building to collect the tickets and passport, rush to the photographer who would swop Goulin's picture for Schwartz's and it would be up the gang-plank and homeward bound. There was just one hitch. How to dispose of Goulin.

At first Schwartz thought of bribing the two *pousseurs* who propelled the rail-car to St. Laurent to stop at a pre-arranged place where he would leap out of the bushes and kill Goulin.

But he discarded this in favour of poison, to be administered to Goulin by his wife before leaving St. Jean. He calculated that a local poison which took about two hours to take effect would overcome the guard at a certain point between St. Jean and St. Laurent. He would bribe the *pousseurs* to keep their mouths shut and that way he and Mme. Goulin would reach St. Laurent where she would go for the tickets and he hide at the photographer's shop until she arrived with the passport.

The ingenious and audacious plan almost worked. But at the last minute, as Mme. Goulin was offering her husband 'one for the road', he saw her fumble with the poison. He beat his wife until she blurted out the whole story and Schwartz was arrested.

Now Goulin had a real problem. The plan was brilliant. But it involved the head warder's wife. And the Administration did not want a scandal. News of it might reach France and that would never do.

So Schwartz was given a severe beating and sentenced to a year in the 'bear pits' of St. Joseph for *évasion*. Technically it was true: he had been planning an escape.

The details were kept secret. It did not matter if Schwartz talked to a few of his fellows. No one would seriously believe the word of a man who assaulted and chopped up little girls.

Goulin and his wife sailed for France as if nothing had happened.

After my third month on 'Route Zero' I tried to break up a fight between two convicts and was severely beaten for my trouble. The three of us were hauled back to St. Laurent and then given a term in Charvin, one of the punishment camps deep in the bush.

Here we worked naked, hacking down the iron-hard timber and cutting it into the log lengths that made up a *stère*. At night we were given back our red and white striped rags and then shackled together in wooden huts. Other men worked at making *bardots*, little roofing boards used in lieu of tiles. The task set was fifty a day. Failure to complete it meant a whipping or worse.

Guards who had fallen out with the Administration were also

sent to Charvin and they took out their frustrations on us. But some of the Corsican guards had volunteered for duty because here they could use their sadistic inclinations to the full.

I saw men buried up to the neck in the damp jungle soil, with only their heads above ground, and left there for twenty-four hours. All day the sun beat down on their shaven skulls and the ants and the mosquitoes had a field day. Usually when a man had gone through this he was quite mad for several days. And some never recovered. Sometimes a man who had angered a warder was stripped, coated with damp sugar and tied to a tree near an ant hill. Others were tied to trees and left there for two or three days. When they were freed they were a mass of insect bites many of which became infected.

A week after I arrived at Charvin I witnessed an incident which showed me exactly what I could expect from the camp.

A guard was beating one of the convicts with a heavy stick for some minor infraction of the rules when the man suddenly turned on him. Before anyone could interfere the convict had beaten the guard's face into a bloody pulp with a piece of wood. He died the same evening.

Officially the convict should have been taken back to St. Laurent for trial. But this was Charvin which often made its own laws.

Instead he was taken into the jungle, manacled to a tree and flogged until his back was raw. Then he was left. Two days later he was still there and his back was alive with ants, maggots and other insects. He shouted for water, begged the guards to kill him and tried to beat his brains out against the tree. At night his agonised cries echoed across the camp where we stirred restively in our huts. On the third day the chief warder visited him. Almost too weak to talk, the man begged for water and was refused. He cursed the French; he cursed the guards; he cursed the mother who had borne him; and finally he cursed God.

Then he died.

At Charvin, strangely, we were paid.

If we survived, and if we could get it from the corrupt Administration, we earned 3f. 20c. a day—about one fifth of what it cost to keep us.

Subsequently I was transferred to Godebert, like Charvin a punishment camp. We worked naked there, too, and received our clothes back at night. Technically Godebert was a camp of *concessionnaires—transportés* hired out to a civilian contractor for work in the lumber yards. We worked from six in the morning until five at night, dragging the heavy trees from the jungle to be sawn into logs. Officially we were only supposed to be let out as *concessionnaires* for six months at a time. But many of the men served terms of six months merely for displeasing a guard.

It was the hell camp of *le bagne*, as much feared as Charvin, but the work was even harder.

Men did terrible things in their frantic efforts to get away from Godebert. They deliberately injured themselves in ghastly ways so that they would be sent to hospital. I know of one convict who jabbed a pin into his right eye. Another rubbed sperm into his eyes and became terribly infected.

We were literally beasts of burden. Harnessed two by two we dragged the heavy timber out of the forest to be cut up. The contractor paid the Government four francs a day for us. If a man died there was always a list of recalcitrants who could be sent to replace him. They brought in water buffaloes to help in the work. But the contractors favoured the buffaloes above the convicts. If a buffalo was hurt or became ill it was rested. If a convict became ill he was worked until he dropped and then a demand for a replacement was sent to the Administration. The buffaloes were worth five or six hundred francs. The convicts were worth nothing.

I took six months at Godebert and should have been returned to St. Laurent. But I had angered one of the Corsican guards and he laughingly told me that he had torn up my papers.

I was desperate. I cried all night, finding strength for tears which I did not know I had. Finally I hit upon a solution. The next morning I took my axe and when the guards were looking the other way I cut open the calf of my right leg; that night I prised open the wound and rubbed excreta into it. A week later, with my leg swollen like a balloon from the infection, I was returned to St. Laurent.

The doctors in *le bagne* were on posting from the French Army and did two-year terms in Guiana. In truth there was little they could do with disease all around and an inadequate supply of drugs.

I was put into the hospital but after a few days my condition was pronounced as incurable. I was too emaciated to survive an operation and blood poisoning was setting in. The doctor told me that I would die under the operating knife, but that I might live for a month at New Camp.

The name struck fear into my heart for New Camp was called *Le Camp des Morts*—Camp of the Dead—and the Camp of Miracles, because it was a miracle if the men sent there came out alive. Officially it was the place where convicts too sick to work were sent to die. There was a New Camp for *relégués* and one for *transportés.*

They sent me there and, indeed, I nearly died. Only the ministrations of a convict named Jacques Lefarge, who was dying of tuberculosis, saved me. He had been an orderly in the hospital at St. Laurent until he contracted TB. He filled me up with *tafia* and then sliced my leg open and took out the pus. He knew all sorts of bushes which contained iron and made vile stews which I drank in my delirium and which undoubtedly saved my life.

When I became strong enough to lie outside our hut I was horrified by what I saw. The sick, the crippled and the insane lived together. The few fit men, sent to the camp to do the heavy work, gave us a wide berth. To be sent to the Camp of the Dead to labour was like a sentence of death. They lived apart from us sick and dying who were everywhere. I looked at the distorted syphilitics, the lumbering victims of elephantiasis, the drooling lunatics, the monsters with ankylostomiasis, and knew that I was in the antechamber to hell.

At New Camp the deaths were not even registered. A doctor occasionally called at the camp but there was little he could do for most of the men. He noted how many were there and reported to the Administration who made a record in their registers, subtracted it from the last count and noted that so many convicts had died. That was all.

Years later I saw a report written by Captain Charles Pean, the Salvation Army officer in charge of the mission to *le bagne*, in which he wrote about New Camp.

'Here the seriously ill, the epileptics, and the imbeciles lived without hope in a misery that beggars description,' Pean wrote. 'Greater misery than this could hardly be imagined. Here two hundred and sixty-eight men were dying—if such a word may be used to describe the end of these beings who were eaten through and through with disease.

'Two of the huts resounded with the throaty rattle of consumptives whose waxen faces, drained of all colour, were contorted by each paroxysm of coughing. Farther on was a hut containing the cripples, the armless, the legless who, lying around all day, passed the time in an exchange of obscenities. In yet another hut were more dying men. Stretched on their foul straw mattresses were paralytics, disfigured syphilitics, and one man with cancer of the face but without any bandage to cover his running sores.'

My friend Lefarge was getting worse and insisted that I move out of the hut so that I stood less chance of contracting his tuberculosis. I built a brush shack nearby and watched the life in the camp while I waited for my leg to heal. I had already gained some weight, and the potions Lefarge continued to brew, and the stews he made from local roots I gathered, were filling and, it seemed, nutritious.

Everything about New Camp was ghastly, but by far the worst feature of it was the presence of the *mômes*. Diseased and disfigured, they dragged their twisted bodies around, managing to swing their hips even when they were on crutches, and painted their ghastly apologies for faces right up to the end.

Lefarge died in my arms and I buried him behind his hut. A few days later the doctor came to the camp and I presented myself to him and showed him my nearly healed leg. He was surprised, but agreed to take me back to St. Laurent with him.

CHAPTER FIVE

THE DOCTOR WAS impressed by my recovery and applied for me to be made a medical orderly at the hospital. He was especially interested in the various local potions that Lefarge had used and questioned me closely about them. I could not help much as I had been delirious when most of them had been used on me.

In the middle of 1928 he took me to the colony's capital at Cayenne to talk to civilian doctors there and to try to identify, from pictures in books, some of the plants.

While I was in Cayenne there was a riot, one of the two which I saw while serving my time in *le bagne*. This one, oddly, was a civilian riot. I pieced together the story from gossip after the actual trouble.

Jean Galmont was the popular Deputy for French Guiana in the French Parliament for many years. He was the popular Mayor of Cayenne for even longer. And then, in 1928, popular Monsieur Galmont was poisoned—hence the riot.

Galmont, born in the Dordogne in 1879, the son of a schoolmaster, became a journalist before entering politics and went to French Guiana as the Deputy in 1919. Apparently he was fond of two things above all else: women and money, in that order. He lived at the rate of £5,000 a year, but earned only £500. Eventually, when his debts were piling up faster than he could stall his creditors, he evolved an ingenious swindle.

Posing as a 'Rum King' he persuaded banks in France and England to lend him money, offering as security a vast amount of rum which he alleged was stored in a warehouse at Bayonne. His financial trickery brought him into contact with the notorious Serge Alexandre Stavisky, already celebrated in financial circles both as a monetary wizard and a swindler. It was never established exactly how much money Galmont succeeded in borrowing, because he extended his activities to influential politicians and prominent businessmen who, when the bubble burst, were far from anxious to come forward and admit that they too had been taken in by the smooth-talking Deputy.

In April, 1921, his run of luck came to an end. A bank laid fraud charges against Galmont and the Chamber of Deputies was forced to withdraw the diplomatic privilege which would otherwise have protected him from arrest.

Galmont was returned to France in disgrace but his political and business contacts got together to have the case side-tracked, many of them fearing that if he ever got into a witness box he would give details and name names which were both important and dishonest.

He returned to Guiana in triumph, his popularity having, if anything, grown during his absence. But while in France he had fallen in love with model Arlette Simon, and formed a hatred based on jealousy for financier Serge Stavisky.

In 1926 Galmont heard from France that the financier was going to marry Arlette Simon. Immediately he secretly denounced Stavisky for fraud—and he had all the proof, having been close to the financier in some of the biggest undercover deals he pulled off. Police investigating Stavisky discovered that he already had convictions for fraud dating back to 1912 and 1915.

A detective named Pachot, who had investigated the earlier Galmont scandal, was the man who arrested Stavisky. According to him the financier immediately realised who had denounced him.

'Where is Galmont?' he demanded. 'He's the one who squealed on me. I will get him later.'

His reason for the denunciation, Galmont told Pachot, was simple.

'I am in love with Arlette Simon,' he said. 'I could not allow her to be taken away by this gang and that little dago Stavisky.'

But Galmont reckoned without the very people who had protected him from prison during his own fraud investigation. They were in with Stavisky just as deeply as they had been with Galmont and they worked just as hard, for the same reasons, to get Stavisky freed. And they succeeded. Stavisky went back to his old tricks nursing a memory of Galmont's treachery. He married Arlette Simon and began to build another financial empire. But all the time he was planning to deal with the Deputy for Guiana.

On 6 August, 1928, Jean Galmont was found dead. The doctors said it was poison, probably arsenic. But when a post-mortem was due to be held it was found that certain vital and tell-tale organs were missing from the body.

Immediately, a riot broke out in Cayenne. The popular Deputy still had his friends and the mob which seethed through the city's streets sought out his political enemies and killed six of them in a bloody orgy of murder.

Libérés following in the wake of the enraged mob looted indiscriminately and I heard it said later, with considerable justification, that many *libéré* restaurants and bars were established and furnished with money stolen during the post-Galmont looting.

The police arrested many men close to Galmont and several who were known to be connected with Stavisky.[1] Forty-five were sent to France and the trial at Nantes dragged on for weeks before all the accused were acquitted.

I was taken back to St. Laurent soon after the riot. My life as a medical orderly was not as tightly controlled as it had been when I was just another convict and I used this added freedom to formulate rough plans for an escape bid if the opportunity presented itself.

Dutch Guiana was obviously out of the question because they returned convicts to the prison authorities. Until 1923 nobody was sent back, but in that year a convict named Cutancot committed a singularly bloody crime when he murdered a complete family and after that every escaped prisoner was sent back. The

[1] Stavisky who, it would seem, had engineered the murder, went from strength to strength and finally, with the exposure of a £6,000,000 fraud hanging over his head, killed himself in his Alpine retreat at Chamonix in January, 1934.—C.R.

country was a haven only for German *évadés*—escapees. Most of them were former Foreign Legionaires and the German Government had an arrangement with the Dutch that their nationals would be returned to Germany—provided that they could prove that they were Germans. This took months and meant the *évadé* filling in a most detailed questionnaire sent from Berlin after the Germon Consul in Paramaribo—the capital of Dutch Guiana—had notified his Government of the alleged birthplace of the alleged German. The questionnaire, with meticulous Teutonic thoroughness, called for detailed answers about the surrounding area of the man's claimed birthplace. If every answer was not correct the man was said not to be a German and was returned to *le bagne* by the Dutch authorities.

In the meantime I took the trouble to learn about *le bagne* and some of the camps in the interior.

About this time they closed the camp at Silver Mountain, far back in the jungle where the convicts worked at cutting wood which was too far away from anywhere to be worth the hauling. Hundreds of *stères* of wood which cost scores of lives just rotted where they were piled.

In Camp des Malagasies the French colonial convicts from the islands of Réunion and Madagascar also worked at cutting wood. They were better fitted to the climate than any of the other convicts, but that was as far as their fitment went. They slaved from dusk to dawn chopping the wood into regular lengths, soul-destroying work at the best of times.

There was also a leper colony in *le bagne*. It was situated on St. Louis Island, well upriver from the coast. At the St. Louis Camp, on the shore opposite the leper island, two hundred convicts worked at planting potatoes. It was also the centre to which convict lepers were taken before being rowed across to the leper island, and the starting point for the one doctor who looked after them, when and if he felt like it. More often than not it was his assistant—a convict—who went to the island. The lepers' food was rowed across daily and thrown on to the shore. After that they were left to divide it among themselves and cook it as they pleased.

Later, there was Inini, a bush camp established in 1930 to house two hundred Cantonese riflemen who had revolted and killed fifty-three French officers in the Yen Bay revolt in Indo-China. In a country infested with snakes, Inini boasted more snakes than most of the other camps put together.

And there was Oyapoc, the most easterly camp in *le bagne*, right on the border of Brazil.

Off the coast lay Les Isles du Salût—the Islands of Salvation—Isle St. Joseph, Isle Royale and Devil's Island.

On St. Joseph were the punishment blocks—known as the 'bear pits'—reserved for *evadés* who had been recaptured, and for convicts found guilty of serious crimes in the Settlements and sentenced to further punishment. The lunatic asylum was also on the island.

Discipline on Isle Royale was tough, but not as strict as on St. Joseph. Convicts who had done time in the 'bear pits' put in a period on Royale before being returned to the mainland.

Then there was Devil's Island, for political prisoners only. Food was sent across from St. Joseph in buckets suspended on a wire.

In a sense there was a fourth island prison—that of *l'Enfant Perdu*—the Lost Child. On this tiny rock, three miles off the shore, was a beacon tended by three convicts who were visited weekly by a small boat bringing their supplies.

At one time only two convicts had tended the light, but during a particularly bad storm one of them went out of his mind, throwing himself at his companion and trying to strangle him, and screaming that the sharks were about to get him. The other man broke away and subdued the madman with an iron bar. When he came round he was still mad and flung himself into the sea.

After that the authorities put three men on the rock to tend the light. But one week their rations were overlooked and when the

Administration launch went out to them after fourteen days, one was completely mad, one had died of hunger and the third died in hospital shortly after his return to the mainland.

On the evening of 28 September, 1928, I went with the doctor to attend to a civilian who had been badly injured by a shark while fishing in the Maroni. It was unusual procedure for the prison doctor to be called out, but the local doctor was drunk and the fisherman was losing blood very fast.

I do not know whether he died or not. We went to the dockside hut to which he had been carried and the doctor examined the injured leg. After a few minutes he sent me back to the camp to bring some instruments for him and when I returned he was too busy to notice me. I had seen the fisherman's boat drawn up by the wharf and the lights of Albina twinkled invitingly to me across the river. There lay freedom. It was a good boat and in a moment of sheer impulse I walked softly away from the crowd of interested onlookers, climbed down into it and pushed off from the shore.

It was one of those ridiculous things that men do. I had no food supply, no water and no experience in sailing. The tide was running out and the boat was carried with it. As luck would have it I was not picked up by the Galibi light and was fortunate in not being overturned in the dangerous currents where the river water met the open sea.

It took me a long time to summon up the courage to hoist the sail, but when I got it up the little boat sped westward along the coast of Dutch Guiana. I felt like singing. But in my heart was the desperate fear that things had gone too well and that my escape was doomed to failure. I landed on the coast near a settlement the following evening and the Negro fishermen were friendly. It was obvious that they knew what I was but they fed me and nobody informed the local police.

A small trading schooner was anchored off the settlement and the captain seemed pleasant. He was a big jovial Dutchman and readily agreed to my tentative request to take me to Paramaribo, the capital. I gave my little boat to the poor family who had fed me and left on the tide the next day.

In Paramaribo I fell in with another *évadé*, a German small-time thief named Strauss—at least that was the name he was travelling under in the hope of persuading the German consul that he was German and therefore should be returned to his homeland. He was awaiting an answer to the questionnaire that he had filled in and was technically under the supervision of the Salvation Army. He was, in fact, French and I gathered that he was certain that he had not made a favourable impression on the consul and that his answers to the questions he had been asked—although he had indeed lived in Germany—would be found to be unsatisfactory. I told him that I was going to push on to Venezuela because they did not send *évadés* back from there and he immediately wanted to join me. We stowed away on another trading schooner which was bound for the Dutch West Indian islands of Curaçao and Aruba but which was due to put in at La Guaira, a Venezuelan port, on the way. Naturally we were discovered the next day when the ship was at sea, but the Dutch captain was friendly and agreed to leave us in Venezuela when he docked. His only stipulation was that if we were picked up that we should not say how we had reached the country.

I managed to get a job working in a waterfront bar and Strauss became a cleaner in a hotel. The seaport was full of escaped convicts but the Venezuelan police took very little notice of them as long as they kept out of trouble. I had not really given a great deal of thought about the future, being content for the time being to earn a meagre living and keep out of the hands of the police.

In two years I managed to save some money and was ready to establish myself in a small business in Caracas, the capital. I had only been there about a week when the dream of a new free life was shattered.

Restive military men plotting to kill the tyrant dictator Gomez—who was at the time out of office, having put another man in the President's chair—hired an *évadé* named Sasse to assassinate the general. The plot was discovered and crushed and Gomez's secret police began mopping-up operations. Their first recommendation was that all former inmates of French Guiana be returned forthwith.

Nearly three hundred *évadés*, myself and Strauss included, were rounded up and imprisoned while the Venezuelan Government contacted the French authorities in Cayenne. Gomez demanded that the Administration send for us and promised to hand back any other escapees who might reach Venezuela in the future. But the Administration was slow in sending a ship to collect us and when it did arrive—eighteen months after the request that we be removed—Gomez demanded a high 'board and lodging' charge for each man. The ship's captain explained that he was not empowered to make such a deal and returned to French Guiana empty. Gomez decided to recoup some of his losses by using us as a chain-gang.

We were put to work building a road from Caracas to Ciudad Bolivar, a big town east of the capital. At first it was a relief from the monotony of the prisons which had been damp and rat-infested. The food was better, too, and I put on some weight as we hacked our way through the bush heading south-east.

Then suddenly, and for no reason that I know of, the whole pattern of our existence changed. A heavy iron ball was attached to our ankles and the quality of the food changed for the worse. It was hard to wield an axe with fifty-six pounds of iron dragging behind you, but we did as well as we could. The anklet which attached the ball and chain chafed my leg and produced ugly sores but in time the skin hardened. Then the machinery which had accompanied us when we started out from Caracas disappeared. We were now expected to build the road almost with our bare hands. It was 'Route Zero' all over again. New guards replaced the old ones and brought a wave of tyranny to the chain-gang road builders. I saw convict labourers shot by brutal guards—some of whom made *le bagne's* Corsicans look like clergymen—'just to see how a Frenchman jumps'.

Eventually we finished the road and were shipped back to Caracas. When we began we were three hundred. When we finished we were sixty-five. Strauss was among the dead. We rotted in a prison for about a month and then one morning we were marched aboard a small freighter and sent back to *le bagne*.

It was the end of my dream of freedom.

CHAPTER SIX

SO I WENT back from Venezuela and in a strange way I was glad. Nothing, I told myself, could be as bad as Gomez's chain gangs. Even the memories of *le bagne* had blurred. My appearance in court lasted just four minutes and I was sentenced to a year on Isle St. Joseph for my escape.

I was put at once into one of the infamous 'bear pits', a cage twelve feet long and seven wide with concrete walls twelve feet high topped by a grill of iron bars. Every cell had a small iron door for passing buckets and food in and out. There were no windows. Overhead, the guards paced a catwalk, watching us when passing over our cells. A tin roof high up shed tropical cloudbursts and collected the heat like an oven.

There were eighty cells in five sheds. We each had a wooden bench six feet long, a blanket, and two wooden buckets, one for food, one as a latrine. There was always plenty of room for more convicts on St. Joseph. Men died like flies in the blistering heat of the 'bear pits' and twice a day the island boat put to sea to toss the bodies to the sharks.

We were forbidden to talk to the men in the neighbouring cells, to the trusties or to the guards. For an hour every day we were taken out and exercised before being returned to the cells. If a man talked to himself he was taken out and whipped for 'creating a disturbance'.

Escape from the 'bear pits' was impossible. The only hope was the hospital. Men did awful things to try to make themselves ill. They beat their heads against walls, tried to hang themselves from the bars, drank their own urine and coolly broke limbs. Another, and more dangerous way, of faking disease was to get a man with tuberculosis to spit into a capsule during the exercise period. The capsule was then sealed up. Then the man with the capsule reported sick complaining of a cough. When the doctor told him to spit he broke the capsule with his teeth before doing so. It was a sure way of getting to the hospital. But at what risk!

Small wonder that men went mad on the Isles of Salvation.

On St. Joseph was the madhouse, where men whose minds had gone were locked away until they died. The violent ones were chained to their bunks for days at a time, only to become more violent as soon as they were unchained. The non-violent ones, naked in case they might rip up their clothes and try to hang themselves, babbled incessantly to each other or screamed out in terror of some imagined disaster.

I was in the hospital for a while because my Venezuelan venture had weakened me to the point of death and the doctor currently doing a two-year stint on St. Joseph was a humane man. If it had not been for him I am certain that I would have died. He saw to it that I received milk and even an occasional egg, the first I had seen since leaving France more than ten years before.

One afternoon there was a terrible row outside the hospital and then a convict was dragged in bleeding profusely. After he had been cleaned up the guards took him back to his cell.

I was well enough by this time to be curious and asked the attendant what was going on. The orderly knew all the gossip—possibly he got some of it from the doctor's files—and told me about the man, Lanio by name.

As a small boy he had been abandoned in Paris by his mother who went off with a man. His father had been killed in an accident some months before. He was sent to a private waifs and strays institution who put him out to work with a farmer. A few weeks later, to escape beatings and continual drudgery, the eight-year-old boy ran away. Almost immediately he was caught and sent to a reformatory. As soon as he was let out he was in trouble again and back he went. His life became a pattern of months in reformatories, days of liberty, and then more months and later years in reformatories. When he was eighteen he was drafted into one of the disciplinary battalions of the French North African Army.

One day he had a fight with a corporal and was thrown into the military dungeons at Biribi with a five-year sentence to complete. He escaped and went to Paris and when the gendarmes came to fetch him he shot one dead. That got him a life sentence in *le bagne*, but even then, while awaiting transportation to St. Martin-de-Ré, he escaped from the prison at Fontevrault with three other convicts. They were soon recaptured and in 1931 were on board *La Martinière* bound for Guiana.

Tattooed in bold letters on Lanio's chest were the words *Enfant du Malheur*—Child of Misfortune.

Several days after the orderly had told me about Lanio the island erupted into violence and the machine guns chattered out their message of death at noon.

Lanio and several other lifers had attacked a guard in a desperate bid to take over the prison. The guard had been killed but their revolt failed when other guards arrived and opened fire on the insurgents. The mutineers were killed and the revolt was put down. But the guards were not taking any chances and security measures were tightened up.[1] The men were kept in their cells for a week before being allowed out to work. It had little effect on me as I was flat on my back in bed.

The medical orderly had a fund of stories and liked to talk to me. One afternoon he talked about Alexander Jacob, the man the 'bear pits' could not break.

Jacob was an anarchist and had led a gang in Paris at the turn of the century. In 1905 he was sentenced to life in Guiana for his part in a battle between the police and anarchists in which a policeman was killed.

He sailed for *le bagne* on 10 November, 1905, determined that he would not be a prisoner for long. A year later he ran through the jungle to where he had hidden a small canoe. Guards were waiting for him and he got thirty days in the cells. For his next bid he chose two veteran convicts and planned a detailed escape. But when he left his hut and headed for the forest the guards

[1] René Belbenoit, who knew Lanio, told pretty much the same story in his book *Dry Guillotine*.

were waiting again. One of his companions had talked. On a third occasion Jacob and two companions reached a raft and were about to put to sea when guards appeared on the shores and called on them to either come back or be shot to pieces. Reluctantly Jacob returned and was sent back to St. Joseph for further punishment.

Now he was considered unbreakable. Guarded closely day and night, he preserved his sanity by planning his next escape when they returned him to St. Laurent. This time, instead of the break-out and a mad dash across the compound to the jungle, Jacob chose to tunnel his way to freedom. But when he opened a trap-door on the end of the tunnel the guards were waiting again. Back he went to the 'bear pits'. He was manacled hand and foot during the whole of his term in the cells. Not because he could escape—a break-out from the 'bear pits' had never been tried for it was an impossibility—but merely to break his spirit. The authorities were successful; it was a weak and emaciated Jacob who was returned to St. Laurent on a stretcher. He would not be in a good enough shape to plan an escape for some time.

When he was released from the hospital he was put on light duties and had the freedom of the camp. He was still too weak to travel and presented no threat to the authorities. Nearly two years of sickness had wasted him to a mere seven stone and dysentery had weakened him beyond recognition.

But he still had his fighting spirit and when he found a particularly brutal Corsican guard walking alone by the Maroni it took him only a moment to stick a knife between his ribs and toss him into the pirana-infested river.

In twenty years Alexander Jacob made eighteen escape bids—all of them unsuccessful. And then in 1925 he changed his tactics. Sent back to St. Laurent, he became a model prisoner who never incurred the slightest displeasure of the guards. His duties were carried out with a complete thoroughness and efficiency and his conduct was near perfect. Three years later he applied for a pardon. Surprisingly enough he got it. On 30 December, 1928, he sailed for home. He had been in Guiana for twenty-three years, nine of them in solitary confinement.[1]

After I came out of hospital I was put to work building, rebuilding and grading the road round the island. It was never used, as there were no vehicles on St. Joseph, but it gave us something to do and was better than the 'bear pits'.

Across from us was Devil's Island, home of the political prisoners. A narrow channel divided the islands, and it boiled white and angry.

But even the roughness did not deter warders from ordering men to dive into it on more than one occasion.

The steel line which linked the islands snapped during a storm and the following day a warder ordered a convict named Saviory, who was a strong swimmer, to dive into the channel and cross to Devil's Island to bring back the hawser. Saviory protested that the water was too rough at the time but might calm later. The guard drew his pistol and offered the convict a choice: dive in and swim or stay where he was and be shot. Saviory dived. His head appeared above the boiling sea for a moment and then he was sucked under. The warder who had deliberately ordered him to dive in was not punished and Saviory's name was entered in the ledgers as 'lost at sea'.

Once a month the cable was greased by volunteer convicts who risked their lives to swing out along its length with an oily rag. If they finished the job—and many did not—they received two bottles of cheap wine and three ounces of tobacco. There was never a shortage of volunteers.

After spending fifteen years on Devil's Island traitors—even lifers—who had not incurred any extra punishment—or gone mad and been taken to St. Joseph's grim asylum—were permitted to return to the mainland and live in Cayenne as *libérés*. But they could never return to France.

My friend, the talkative medical orderly, suddenly went down with appendicitis and the doctor requested that I be made

[1] Alexander Jacob committed suicide in Paris in 1954 at the age of seventy-one. —C.R.

temporary orderly to replace him. The request was granted and I found myself back in a white coat again. A week later I accompanied the doctor on the fortnightly boat to Devil's Island itself. On this occasion a priest came with us.

The prisoners prepared the food that was sent over from St. Joseph and lived in separate little huts. I envied them, for they did no work, received newspapers and magazines and in many ways their life was not unpleasant.

Their chief enemy was boredom.

The most famous traitor on Devil's Island at that time was Georges Richard, the man who had betrayed Nurse Edith Cavell to the Germans during the First World War. She had established an escape system for Allied troops which had spirited scores of men back to the Allied lines after capture by the enemy. But Richard betrayed her and in October, 1915, the Germans took Nurse Cavell out and shot her at dawn. The betrayer was convicted of treason in 1919 and sent to *le bagne* for the rest of his life.

I hoped that I would catch a glimpse of him.

A rough path which ran the length of the island separated the huts of the men. It was known as Traitors' Lane and Richard lived at the end of it. None of the men on the island had clean consciences—but none of them would speak to Richard. And I noticed that even the guards who accompanied us and inspected the huts hated him. They did not even bother to curse him.

It had been the same when he first arrived at St. Laurent and his name and crime had become public knowledge. A convict had tried to knife him but was beaten off by the guards. After that Richard's life was not safe for the short time that he was held at the Camp de le Transportation pending imprisonment on Devil's Island.

And so, for nineteen years, until his death in 1938, Georges Richard spoke to no one—or if he did they did not answer him. He was the loneliest man in *le bagne*.

The doctor told me the story of Henri Bellon, like Dreyfus convicted for treason and sent to Devil's Island for life, And, like Dreyfus, innocent.

Bellon, then twenty-two, joined the French Army at the outbreak of the First World War. Almost immediately he was wounded and invalided out, returning to Marseilles to his hairdressing salon. The following year he went to Geneva on business and while there met Stanley Mitchell, an American citizen, who was a Pole by birth. Mitchell told Bellon that he was in the French counter-espionage service keeping track of the many German and Turkish spies who were using Switzerland's neutrality to assist them in their chosen profession. He explained that his spoken French was good enough to get him around, but that his written French was bad and he was having difficulty with his reports to the espionage chiefs. He asked Bellon to help him. The pair worked closely for several months and then suddenly the Swiss police swooped on Mitchell and deported him as a spy. Back in Paris Mitchell reported to his chiefs that Bellon had denounced him and a warrant was served on the hairdresser as he crossed the border back into France.

In the autumn of 1915 he found himself on a treason charge being heard before a military court. He pleaded not guilty, maintaining that he was a loyal French citizen, who had been wounded in the service of his country, and brought evidence into court to show that he had been in Geneva on legitimate business. He had in fact been making contacts with wig-makers and hairnet manufacturers.

Stanley Mitchell testified against Bellon. His evidence was entirely circumstantial and much of it was merely hearsay. But there was a war going on. The military judges reasoned that Mitchell had been a fairly valued agent who, until Bellon's arrival, had been turning in useful information. He appeared to have no axe to grind against the Marseilles hairdresser and there was at least a possibility that some foreign power could have added Bellon to their payroll as a counter-counter-espionage agent.

Bellon was sentenced to life imprisonment and reached Guiana in 1916.

One day in 1925 he read a three-month-old copy of the Paris

newspaper *Le Matin* and his disinterested eye ran over a murder story involving one Lazare Tissier who was charged with killing a man in the Bois de Boulogne. Bellon was not very interested in murder trials, but he made it a point to read every word in the few newspapers he received. After all, he had plenty of time to kill until the next batch came. Suddenly he saw a name that meant everything to him: Stanley Mitchell. Feverishly Bellon turned back to the beginning of the murder trial report. Lazare Tissier, a caretaker, was on trial for his life charged with the murder of a bookmaker named Bellay. The prosecution had established a motive for the crime and had an almost watertight case against him. The only weak point was how he could have got Bellay's body to the Bois de Boulogne where it had been found.

At this juncture Stanley Mitchell stepped into the story claiming that he had seen Tissier pushing the body in a wheelbarrow. Mitchell explained that he had been released from prison the day before the murder. He said he had spent the night sleeping rough and had then gone for an early morning walk in the Bois. He claimed that Tissier had passed close by him with Bellay's body. At the time Mitchell was under a deportation order having run up a long record of petty crimes. He was anxious to reinstate himself in the eyes of the French authorities and made his testimony as black as possible for Tissier. Fortunately he made such an unfavourable impression on the trial judge that his evidence was ruled out of the proceedings.

Immediately after reading the newspaper story Bellon sat down and wrote a long letter to the Ministry of Justice, pointing out that he had been convicted of treason solely on Mitchell's rather dubious evidence and requesting a new trial. Mitchell had by then been deported from France and the Minister felt it fair and reasonable to comply with Bellon's request.

At the new trial the Public Prosecutor simply announced that there had been a judicial error and quashed Bellon's sentence. He sailed for France, arriving at Le Havre on 1 April, 1929—

thirteen years after he had been sent in chains and disgrace to Devil's Island. He was given £40 compensation.

Only once as far as I know was there an escape bid made from Devil's Island itself. A plan was conceived by four men who spent months building a boat from pieces of driftwood in a trench dug out under the floor of one of the concrete huts. While they were building the boat they lived on half rations, saving tins of condensed milk, medical stores and bread, which they toasted, for their sea journey. Then, on the night they were to leave, they discovered that the boat they had built was bigger than the doorway of the hut. Frantically, they breached the wall and ran down to the rocks to put off.

Hours later they were no more than a dozen yards from where the sea was breaking whitely on the jagged shore. Their fevered paddling was making no headway against the swell, merely holding them off the rocks. Finally an extra large wave lifted the boat high and sent it crashing in a splintered wreck on the shore. The four men dragged themselves back to their huts totally exhausted. The following day they were transferred to St. Joseph to undergo punishment for having destroyed Government property—the wall they had breached to get the boat out of the hut.

After a year on St. Joseph I was transferred to Isle Royale before being sent back to the mainland.

The main cellblock on the island was painted red and was naturally known as *La Case Rouge*—the Bloody Barracks. It contained long, extremely narrow cells, probably about forty feet by six, into which as many as eighty men were crammed. In some ways it reminded me of the cages on *La Martinière*. There was a lavatory at each end of the cell and it was not uncommon for a man to be found dead in one of them in the morning, knifed for the contents of his *plan*.

I had three months on Royale before being returned to St. Laurent.

On the day that I was to be transferred to the mainland I was taken to the Administration building to obtain my papers. The man who attended to me was Guy Davin, one of the most favoured convicts in *le bagne*. His father was a guard.

In December, 1931, Richard Wall, an American who lived in Paris, was found floating in the Seine at Mousseaux. He had been shot. An ugly bullet hole in his neck indicated that the gun had been held close to his head before being fired and police began questioning his associates. Suspicion pointed at Guy Davin, a wealthy young socialite, but he denied any knowledge of the crime. Circumstantial evidence was strong but the police had nothing conclusive until they discovered some bloodstained and partly burned clothes halfway between Triel and Poissey. They belonged to Davin. Under interrogation he broke down and was charged with murder. His counsel recommended that he plead guilty to save himself from the gu illotine. He was sentenced to life imprisonment in Guiana and arrived in 1932.

Davin's father, the *le bagne* guard, had been involved in a scandal in high circles and to save himself from prison in France had bought a job in the Penal Administration. He took the first opportunity to talk to his son and promised to use his influence to try to ease his lot. And he was as good as his word. Davin was never sent to the wood-cutting or rock-breaking camps where men died like flies. Instead, he found himself living a life of luxury on Isle Royale as secretary to the island's Director. He lived in the Director's house, wore civilian clothes and was allowed to receive money from his wealthy family in France.

Soon after I left Isle Royale news reached the mainland Settlements of Davin's death.

Even though he lived in better conditions than most of the men sent out from France to guard him, Davin wanted to escape. He was hated by the convicts and he knew that sooner or later one of them would take a knife to him for the gold fillings in his teeth and the diamond ring on his finger. One night when there was a celebration at *La Salle d'Honneur*—the warders' clubroom—Davin and two companions, Charlot and Vaillant, broke into a storeroom and stole some oil drums to use as floats for a raft. They put out from the island without paddles or any means of steering their raft and within an hour were washed back on to the rocks. A heavy sea was running and their frail craft was smashed to pieces.

Charlot was lost in the sea; Vaillant was badly injured; Davin made it ashore safely. Leaving Vaillant where he lay, Davin made his way back to the Director's quarters undetected.

The next day guards found the injured Vaillant and in the hospital he implicated Davin. Charlot's body, badly mauled by sharks, was washed up later. Davin denied everything, claiming that he was hated by the other convicts, and that Vaillant, knowing that he was dying, implicated him just to get him into trouble. His father pulled strings from inside the Administration and he was released. Vaillant was sent to the cells on St. Joseph for trying to escape but died on the way.

But this time the word was really out for Guy Davin.

A week later his stripped and mutilated body was found in the bush. Gone were his diamond ring, his money—and his gold teeth.[1]

I arrived at St. Laurent just in time to witness my first public guillotining.

The most hated men in *le bagne* were the executioners. There were two of them: one on the Islands and one in the mainland Settlements. They were always convicts, usually convicted murderers, and invariably volunteers drawn from several to fill the place as the most despised and feared men in the penal colony.

In the language of the convicts the executioners were *mouchards*—traitors to their friends, informers—and there was not one of us who would have hesitated to stick a knife between an executioner's ribs given half a chance.

When a new executioner was needed for the colony the

[1] George Seaton saw Davin on Royale and at first took him for a civilian. 'I saw a tall, well-fed young man with long, brilliantined hair and a magnificently cut suit of ducks,' he wrote. 'His shirts and socks were of silk, a diamond glittered on his left hand, his shoes were of doeskin, and his nails were well cared for. An effete, bored-looking socialite, such as one might see in a London bar.'—*Scars Are My Passport*.

assembled convicts were told and a volunteer was asked for. But no man dared step forward. For they knew only too well that if three volunteered and one was chosen the other two would die soon. To the other convicts they would have expressed a willingness to rat on their friends, and after a time they would be found knifed somewhere out in the jungle.

Even so, an executioner could always be found. After the Commandant had called for volunteers he could expect to receive a number of pencilled notes applying for the post and from them he would choose his man.

The Island executioner, hated and feared, protected by the guards, but despised by them at the same time, lived in an isolated hut at the end of Isle Royale. He received special extra rations and clothes and was allowed to carry a sharpened bush knife for defence against attacks. The mainland executioner lived in a separate and guarded hut in St. Laurent and kept fierce dogs for his own protection. He received about £1 for every guillotining and was, by convict standards, a rich man.

The St. Laurent guillotine was a journeyman killing machine, taken down and moved about the Settlements when needed. It was always escorted by the Commandant and a troop of Senegalese soldiers, and when *la veuve gaie* came to a camp it was time for death.

The post of executioner gave a man many advantages over his fellow convicts and if he were violent enough he could feather his own nest under the very noses of the guards.

When I first arrived in *le bagne* the convicts were still talking about executioner Marcel Bonnefoy who had been guillotined a short time before on his own death machine by his successor.

Bonnefoy, using the extra freedom that his position gave him, had evolved an excellent money-making scheme which was foolproof for a time. He would offer to help *évadés* to cross the Maroni into Dutch Guiana for a fee, usually exorbitant. The *évadé* would pay Bonnefoy his fee and then be told to meet the executioner at an appointed place where a canoe would be hidden for the crossing. But once the *évadé* came creeping through the

3. Devil's Island with the Isle St. Joseph in the foreground. The two-storied building on the left of the picture was the hospital, with the iron roofs over the "bear pits" in front of it. The other two-storied building in the picture was the insane asylum.—Associated Press Photo

4. Two elaborately-tattooed convicts photographed in Trinidad in 1938 after escaping from *le bagne* by canoe. There were seven in the party, and they left for Panama in a boat supplied by the Salvation Army in Port of Spain.—Associated Press Photo

undergrowth to his rendezvous Bonnefoy would spring from cover and sink his knife into the man's back, rip him open for his *plan*, and the bury the body.

Bonnefoy killed six *évadés* he was pretending to help escape but was caught at his seventh murder. He chose as the rendezvous the exact place that one of the homosexual guards had arranged to meet his *môme*.

The guard saw Bonnefoy kill the *évadé* and then captured him. He received a reward for capturing the man, Bonnefoy was sentenced to the guillotine, and the *môme* received the contents of the *évadé's plan*.

Marcel Bonnefoy died on his own guillotine at the hand of Leon La Durrell, who had killed his sweetheart in Metz and had arrived in *le bagne* one boatload ahead of me. He was a wispy little man with a ragged unkempt moustache and he took a great pride in his work.

In fifteen years he executed eighteen men including a half-Arab, half-Italian *relégué* named Simonetti who had killed another convict for the fortune rumoured to be hidden in his *plan*. Simonetti had found only five francs and was caught by a guard extracting it. He was a prominent *fort-à-bras* and his execution was remembered for a long time.

There was a macabre thrill in listening to the men talk about the executions that they had seen and apart from that of Bonnefoy I had been told about two others which had stuck in men's minds.

One was a double execution. The first man had come out bravely, but had broken down at the last minute and had had to be dragged to the scaffold and strapped down. The second man when he came out, walked directly to the scaffold and was about to mount the steps when a convict from the assembled crowd dashed forward and flung his arms about him. They were brothers. The one who had rushed forward begged the Commandant to show mercy, but the guards were ordered to drag him away. The brother who was to be executed mounted the scaffold, looked around the assembled convicts and then called out a last farewell before he was strapped down and guillotined.

The other one they talked about was that of a Sicilian *fort-à-bras* who was said to have been one of the toughest men ever sent to *le bagne*. He had killed a guard while escaping and after being sent back from Brazil was sentenced to be executed. The guards were so afraid of him that he, for the first and last time in the history of the guillotining in *le bagne*, was taken to the scaffold in chains.

The knife was dropped and his head rolled into the basket, but so powerful was the man, and so strong his will to rebel, that for many seconds afterwards the body leapt about. The straps that held it down were burst and only the weight of the chains kept it from falling off the scaffold. Blood gushed everywhere and the guards started to run.

But the most terrible sight was the executioner. He was drenched in blood from head to toe.[1]

The man I was to see executed had murdered a guard at the punishment camp of Charvin and had been severely beaten. His name was Kautz, and he was formerly in the French Foreign Legion.

I had seen men killed in fights with knives; seen them flogged to death by warders; seen them die of every tropical disease known to *le bagne*. But I had never seen a man judicially executed and there was a horrid fascination in watching a man die on *la veuve gaie*.

Kautz was brought out flanked by Senegalese troops and guards. He walked with his head high and his puny chest thrust out. Some men took a pride in dying bravely. They lived badly, degraded, beaten, cursed. But something in them made them want to go out on a grand scale. They strapped Kautz to the

[1] The story of this same execution was also told to William Willis, author of *Damned and Damned Again* by an eye witness. It varies from Etienne Artaud's version only in that the murderer is referred to as having been Maltese. 'I'll never forget it,' Willis's informant said. 'The executioner was bathed in the man's blood from head to foot—there was not an inch of him that was not covered. He was really drenched. What a sight around the guillotine. They had a time with us getting us out of the yard—men were half crazy. *Oui, oui*, it was a strange day, and two murders were committed before the sun went down, and that night in the blockhouse the convicts howled like beasts and fought each other with knives.'

guillotine boards and then La Durrell pulled the lever that sent the knife slicing down on the man's neck.

The head jerked downwards and then began to roll towards the basket. I watched horrified, but at the same time riveted to the spectacle. It was a form of mass hypnotism. Not a man among the watching convicts moved. The head balanced for a second on the edge of the board and then dropped into the basket with a dull thud. Blood spurted in all directions and for a moment the body on the board tensed. Then it relaxed and a low murmur ran through the assembled convicts. It was over.

There was no more work that day. After an execution we were always unsettled and were herded back to the barracks under guard.

I was kept at St. Laurent for about six months and dreamed of escape every time I went out with a work party. The Dutch settlement of Albina danced temptingly before my eyes across the Maroni.

CHAPTER SEVEN

EVERY DAY WE went out to cut wood or sweep the streets and in my work party was a man named Lanio—no relative, as far as I know, of the man who tried to start a mutiny on St. Joseph. But he was a tough, undisciplined killer who had led a gang in Paris and was sent to *le bagne* for murdering a policeman.

He had also had the distinction of being the only man ever to start a mutiny aboard *La Martinière*.

It was in December, 1933, while the floating 'black maria' was in mid-Atlantic. The food was terrible and the discipline tougher than ever. Only the year before a journalist named Luc Dornain had stowed away on the prison ship and then written a series of scorching articles for the French Press.

La Martinière had been at sea for nearly two weeks when Lanio and a group of *transportés* in a forward hold grabbed a guard and dragged him into the cage with them. They took his gun and keys and within minutes a full-scale revolt was going on down in the hold.

But one guard escaped and gave the alarm. The steam hoses began to hiss into the cage where some men still remained. Lanio was outside in the gangway between the cages but each one was sealed off from the others as a separate unit and soon the scalding steam had nearly filled the cage. Mutineers and unwilling onlookers alike were scalded. More than forty convicts died and dozens of others were badly burned during the five minutes that the hoses were on. Then down came the guards swinging clubs to deal with the last bit of fight left in the men.

Lanio, though burned, was still fighting at the last and was hurried to the 'hot box' by the boilers for further punishment. He spent the rest of the voyage in irons. The day after the revolt *La Martinière* hove to as forty canvas-wrapped bodies weighted with pig-iron were dumped over the side. Then she sailed on.

Lanio had spent a year in the 'bear pits' on St. Joseph and a further three months on Isle Royale for starting the mutiny. Then he was transferred to St. Laurent.

One morning in April, 1935, we had just marched out of the cookhouse and were being taken to collect our axes from the armoury when Lanio made his last bid for freedom.

He suddenly broke away from the line of convicts and jumped at a guard who had his back to him. He felled the man with a single blow, grabbed his gun and than ran zig-zagging across the parade ground and disappeared between two huts. We were instantly halted and more guards came running with machine guns and covered us to prevent anyone from joining Lanio. We all stood rigidly to attention, aware that the slightest move would make the trigger-happy guards open fire. After five minutes we were herded back to our huts and told to stay inside. Senegalese sentries were posted at the doors with rifles and fixed bayonets.

After about half an hour we heard shots and guessed that they had got Lanio. We learned later in the day that he had managed to grab the child of one of the guards and, using it as a shield, had tried to force his way into the armoury. He killed two Arab trusties who tried to stop him, grabbed several guns and then ran for the river. Another convict joined him in the dash for freedom. There were no boats about so they jumped in and began to swim. The second convict was attacked by a shark only yards from the shore but Lanio kept swimming. He was about halfway across the river when a guard with a high-powered rifle put a bullet into his head.[1]

Three months later, on 10 July, 1935—I shall never forget that day—I was summoned to the Commandant's office and told that my sentence plus the extra year for my escape, was completed and that I could begin my *doublage*. I was a *libéré* at last. I was given three days in which to gather my belongings—as if I

[1] The escape bid was witnessed by French woman lawyer Maître Mireille Maroger, who was visiting St. Laurent at the time, and it gained some Press attention when she returned to France.—C.R.

needed a quarter of that time—and was issued with a new uniform and a blanket.

In those three days I met René Belbenoit, convict and writer, who is probably the best-known of all the one-time inmates of *le bagne*. He had been sent to Guiana in 1923 as a *relégué* at the age of twenty-one. His crime was the theft of a necklace worth less than £100. He made an escape and was sent to the 'bear pits' on St. Joseph. Eventually, in 1930, Governor Siadous did an unheard of thing: he gave Belbenoit a passport and freedom to leave Guiana for a year.[1] He went to the Panama Canal Zone and at the end of his time returned to France and reported to the authorities.

Then, to his amazement, he was charged with escape and sent back on *La Martinière*. When he arrived at St. Laurent they put him in court and he was sentenced to the 'bear pits' again.

He had been writing a book on *le bagne* all the time he was there. While other convicts smoked, swore, gambled, made love and fought in the barracks at night, Belbenoit had been writing. He used bits of paper when he could get them, but often he resorted to pieces of bark, old bits of rag and even the hard shiny leaves of the bigger trees. Whenever he was moved from one camp to another he left his manuscript with friends and collected it later.

When I met him he had just returned from St. Joseph and was very bitter, not without good cause. I never saw him again but I heard two years later that he had escaped and that he had reached America and found sanctuary there. He wrote two books[2] which aroused a lot of feeling about *le bagne* in the outside world.

It was every convict's dream not only to escape but to get to the United States eventually and manage to live there undetected. Now and then *évadés* like Belbenoit, Jean Brabant and Rousseau, men who had got to France and had been sent back, brought

[1] Of the 679 men who had gone to Guiana with Belbenoit in 1923 only fifteen were still alive seven years later.

[2] *Dry Guillotine* (1938) and *Hell on Trial* (1940). Belbenoit died at his home in Nevada in February, 1960.

tales of convicts who had reached America and had then been caught.

I even met one of them, Amatti de Desederio, once famous throughout France as 'The Phantom Bandit'. It took the American immigration men twenty-two years to run him down but eventually he was shipped back to France.

It was 1911 when Desederio made his escape from *le bagne* on a small raft which took him to British Guiana. From Georgetown, the capital, he worked his passage to America on a tramp steamer, jumping ship in New York and vanishing into the metropolitan jungle. Soon he was in trouble again, pursued by the New York police for burglary. Desederio headed west, always one jump ahead of the local police, making his living as a farm labourer in the country and a petty thief in the cities and towns. He remained free until 1933. Then he was arrested for burglary in the Italian quarter of San Francisco. Immigration officials discovered his true identity and back he went to France and ultimately to *le bagne*.

After being released as a *libéré* I hung around St. Laurent for a while scratching for a living. There was little to do and few people would give us work. I knew that if I was picked up for vagrançy I should be in trouble because after three court appearances on this charge a *libéré* was considered not to be trying to work and was automatically made a *relégué* and sent to St. Jean, the big camp far back in the jungle behind St. Laurent. And as a *relégué* a convict was bound to Guiana's prison camps for life. Eventually I found a job digging graves.

We were, in fact, little concerned with cemeteries, for death was always with us, but a section of the cemetery had been allotted for the bodies of *libérés*. If one of us died he was said to have 'Gone to the Bamboos' because a large stand of bamboos separated the weed-grown *libéré* burial ground from the cemetery proper. At least those who were buried there had the satisfaction, if they cared, of knowing that their bodies lay in sacred ground and were not tossed to the sharks as happened on the islands.

But once we grave-diggers had covered the rough plank coffin there was nothing else to do. And there was nobody to mark the graves either unless a friend pencilled the dead man's name on a piece of paper and fixed it with a stick. We diggers did a little weeding and the fence kept back the jungle which for ever seeks to reclaim what man has taken from it.

There was no one who really cared. No one, that is, until The Crazy Nun came to St. Laurent. After that, whenever a *libéré* was buried, The Crazy Nun went to The Bamboos to take a little bunch of flowers and say a prayer for the dead man. She worked as a seamstress for the warders' wives and Government officials, but nobody knew her past. And no one could remember exactly when she arrived—or how.

There were many stories about her. It was said that she had come to *le bagne* seeking a lover who had been sent out from France for petty theft. Another story had her as a nun sent out by a holy order who had fallen in love with a convict and then gone crazy when her man died or escaped. She used to stand by The Black Gate watching the men shuffle past on their way back from work. Then she began to visit the cemetery.

She wore a long black dress and a veil which hid her face and she always carried a prayer book in her white-gloved hands.

There were between fifteen and twenty Catholic priests, authorised by the Governor and paid by the State, at St. Laurent and Cayenne. In theory they were prison chaplains, but in practice they spent more time tending their Negro, Indian and Chinese flock than ministering to the men they had been sent to help. And no man sent to Guiana for a crime—whatever his status in the penal settlements—could enter a Roman Catholic church. If a religiously inclined *libéré* died, the burial cart would be halted near the church door and the priest would sprinkle the corpse with holy water before it was taken to The Bamboos.

Only those condemned to die by the guillotine could receive the last rites.

I stuck the job for a while and then decided to go to Cayenne. I had liked what I had seen of it when taken there to tell the doctors about my experiences of bush medicine in New Camp and I hoped to find work.

I lived in the *libéré* settlement for two months vainly hunting for work. Next door to me was a man named Henri De Bouyn and how he ever became a *libéré* was a mystery to me. For he was an incorrigible escaper.

He had been in the Foreign Legion and had killed a sergeant in a fight over a girl. He had been in *le bagne* for about thirty years when I met him and heard his story.

At first he had been put to work sweeping the streets in Cayenne and soon, by bribing the guards with a cut of the profit, he had worked up a lucrative sideline selling souvenirs carved by himself—he was a talented sculptor—and some other artistic *libérés* to the tourists. Months later, after crushing his thumb while labouring on the wharves, he was transferred to a clerking job in the Administrative building and he wasted no time in locating his own prison dossier, transferring his statistics and number to the 'dead' record cabinet and substituting a dead man's personal details and fingerprints to his own file. A week later he was back on the docks. He got a spell on Isle Royale soon afterwards and when he was transferred to the mainland made plans for an escape. He got to British Guiana and worked on a plantation.

When he was finally sent back he hoped that the destruction of his records would confuse the authorities and encourage them to believe the tale he spun about being a deserter from the Army garrison in Martinique. But a guard recognised him and he was sent to the 'bear pits' on St. Joseph.

As soon as he was returned to the mainland he escaped again. This time he went into the bush in the jungles of British Guiana and married an Amerindian woman. She died four years later and De Bouyn went to Georgetown where he was arrested and sent back to *le bagne*. He was put in the 'bear pits' again.

There was no holding him. His next escape bid was in a canoe. He got to Trinidad and was sent back.

After a month I suggested to De Bouyn that we should go to the Salvation Army hostel and camp on the Montjoly peninsula. At least we could be fed there and would not be charged with vagrancy.

The officer in charge was Captain Charles Pean, a wonderful man. He had been trying to get a mission established in *le bagne* since 1910 but had only succeeded in 1933 so things were still quite new when De Bouyn and I arrived.

* * *

Captain Pean stepped on to the dock at St. Laurent on 25 July, 1928, armed with letters of authority calling upon the Administration to afford him every opportunity to see what *le bagne* was really like. He visited every camp on the mainland and the three Isles du Salût and was appalled by what he saw. He made up his mind to devote his life to the closure of the penal colony.

'The long-term goal is the total abolition of the Penal Settlements,' he wrote in his report to his superiors.

But he knew that it could not be done overnight. In the meantime he suggested a series of schemes which he hoped would give the *libérés* some independence and help them to regain their self-respect. He proposed that first offenders should be separated from the old hands; that individual cells should replace the common barracks; that the system of pardons be reformed; that *doublage* should be abolished; and that a repatriation service should be undertaken by the Salvation Army. For the *libérés* of the colony he suggested a series of measures aimed at giving them a degree of independence as the first way to help them gain their self-respect. He proposed the setting-up of hostels for them at St. Laurent and Cayenne where they could have beds in individual cubicles, a common-room and a restaurant run by the Army. He asked for funds to establish a workshop where craftsmen could make things for sale to the civilian population and the few tourists and keep the hostels in good repair at the same time. Jams could be made locally from the guavas, lemons and pineapples, he reported. A brickfield might be bought to be worked by other *libérés*. And a tannery could be set up.

Most of all he stressed the urgent need for a labour exchange where *libérés* might learn of the few jobs available in the towns and then go to the Army for references which would enable them to apply. He reported that many men with families had lost touch with them and suggested that the Army might become the link between families in France and convicts in *le bagne*. The Army would need three officers in Guiana to begin with and at least two more at a later date.

He finished the report shortly before landing at Le Havre on 12 September, 1928.

Months dragged by and nothing happened. Then, in June, 1929, the Army's National Committee agreed to set up a mission in *le bagne*. Early the following month Commissioner Albin Peyron and a delegation of Members of Parliament called on the Minister for the Colonies requesting Government support for the mission. At the same time Monsieur Maurice Sybille of the Chamber of Deputies suggested modifications in the penal laws which would mean an end to the transportation of all those not subject to permanent banishment and would abolish the compulsory residence clause in the case of the *libérés*. But the proposal, voted on without even a debate, was lost in the parliamentary paper-work and never implemented.

Three years passed. In France the Salvation Army kept up a consistent war of attack on the Government, lobbying Deputies whenever they could find a sympathetic ear. In *le bagne* the year 1930 had ushered in a decade of escapes which would see *évadés* reaching every conceivable part of South and Central America and every island in the Caribbean Sea.

Finally, on 8 February, 1933, after a deputation of Salvation Army officers had called on the Minister for the Colonies, permission was at last granted for the Army to go to *le bagne*. Three months later came official confirmation of the word-of-mouth agreement and on 10 May the *Bureau de Bagne* was established.

Pean, working in close conjunction with Commissioner

Peyron, was instrumental in setting up a consultative committee under the joint-chairmanship of the Ministers for the Colonies, Justice and the Interior, and in co-opting organisations interested in social work to look after the problem of *le bagne*. He embarked on a mammoth lecture tour of France drumming up the financial support that the Army so badly needed. He helped Peyron choose Army personnel—not just the three initial officers he had recommended, but seven.

And on 5 July, after a solemn ceremony, the actual flag that would be unfurled over the first mission was blessed and dedicated. The following day Pean and six officers sailed for French Guiana on the *Antille*, landing at Cayenne after a twenty-four-day voyage.

They went into action immediately. The peninsula of Montjoly, about eight miles west of Cayenne, was leased for the first farm. The Army's flag was unfurled on 25 August. A hostel was established for the *libérés* and the whole place cleared of undergrowth to get the planting under way.

Soon Commissioner Peyron and his daughter Irene—also a Salvation Army officer—arrived for an inspection tour and stayed a month before returning to France to appeal for more funds and more support for the *Bureau de Bagne*.

Pean established in Cayenne *La Maison de France*, a hostel for *libérés*, the following November. Bed and breakfast cost 50 centimes or 1 franc a night. A carpentery shop was set up where the men could work and earn the money they needed to live in the hostel.

Two officers were assigned to the *Maison de France*, two to Montjoly, and Pean took one with him to St. Laurent to establish a hostel there. Everywhere they were met by long queues of *libérés* who wanted to earn enough money during their *doublage* to go home when their terms expired and by *relégués individuals* who had to support themselves for life in the colony.

Pean's suggestions that the Salvation Army should become a link between convicts and their families was put into operation and during the first year they interviewed 5,159 men and their families and wrote 1,032 letters on their behalf.

Pean returned to Paris late in 1934 and from that time on was always journeying between *le bagne* and the French capital. In his absence his officers worked harder than ever. New banana plantations were opened to make the Army's work in *le bagne* self-supporting. Their reports to Paris were eagerly scrutinised by Peyron and Pean who followed every step in the *Bureau de Bagne* with meticulous detail.

Reports were simple. The officers took every minor setback in their stride. 'The officers are well,' said one report; 'The Captain was stung by a vampire which slid under his mosquito net and left him an ugly sore,' said another; 'The Lieutenant had a battle with a snake,' said a third.

The Army began another money-making sideline for the *libérés*. The beautiful Guiana *Morpho-Menelaus* butterflies had long been hunted to sell to tourists for whatever they could get. The same butterflies once sparked off a revolt at St. Jean. Now the Army set a price of 5 francs for every perfect specimen and the men went to work with renewed zeal. Soon moths and reptiles were added to the income-earners and the officers' rooms began to look like taxidermists' offices.

One of the most successful butterfly catchers even managed to get himself released from *le bagne* to make a trip to Europe on parole to establish contacts with buyers and dealers. He was Georges Gutmann, sent to Guiana in 1910 for fraud, who as a *libéré* had worked up a sizeable trade as a dealer in butterflies.

But while in Europe Gutmann spent all his money and did not have his fare back to *le bagne*. He took a job to raise the money and, when the end of his parole neared and he still lacked funds, he stole from his employer. He was arrested and sentenced to four years for the theft but appealed. His sentence was reduced to eighteen months providing that he went back to *le bagne* at once.

The Salvation Army's plans in Guiana were prospering beyond their hopes. But with joy came tears too. Refractory *libérés* took advantage of the officers, used the money they earned to buy rum and get riotously drunk, and destroyed property.[1]

* * *

Captain Pean gave me a job in the carpentry shop and found work for De Bouyn on one of the newly established banana plantations.

A month later the incorrigible escaper fled again, this time northwards into the jungles of French Guiana.

[1] Etienne Artaud was not familiar with the background to the Army's mission in Guiana and I have filled it in. Much of the information is from Captain Charles Pean's book *The Conquest of Devil's Island*.—C.R.

CHAPTER EIGHT

MEN HAD ALWAYS tried to escape from *le bagne* but about 1927 there was a big increase in the number of attempts and during the 1930s hundreds of men made breaks for freedom. They were always being brought back from the jungle or sent back from Dutch Guiana, Brazil, British Guiana and even farther afield. About eight hundred men tried to escape every year, but if one in ten managed to find sanctuary it was a high figure.

We *libérés* at Montjoly were not encouraged to waste time in gossiping about escapers, but of course we did, especially in the evenings after supper.

And there were plenty of stories to tell.

I met Jean Brabant when he was doing his second term in *le bagne*. He had been sent to Guiana in 1902 for armed robbery and in 1907 he became one of the first men to make a successful escape through the jungle to Venezuela.

He became a tailor in Caracas and in time grew very prosperous, holding the contract for supplying uniforms to the army in general and President Gomez in particular. But then he became homesick. In 1928 he became a naturalised Venezuelan and two years later, just before the purge which sent me to the chain gang, booked a passage to Barcelona planning to cross into France and spend a holiday and then return to Venezuela.

On the border, as French police detained him because of slight irregularities in his papers, Brabant's nerve failed. He broke down and confessed that he was an *évadé*. He met René Belbenoit in prison awaiting return to *le bagne*.

One escape had occurred on 28 July, 1930, when I was working in Venezuela, just before all *évadés* in Caracas were rounded up. In its way it was typical of the escapes from *le bagne* by sea, but it had far-reaching consequences.

In the flimsy canoe which slipped past the Galibi Light that night were five men: Cirille Albert Caullier, serving a term of life imprisonment for attempted murder; Pierre Robert Retzenger, sent to *le bagne* in 1919 to serve a sentence of twenty years for a killing; Gregoire Kossekechatko, convicted of a political killing in 1925 and sent to Guiana for ten years; and two other men with similar crimes to their names.

A storm hit the dugout and capsized it when they had been at sea for four days and two of the men were drowned. Caullier, Retzenger and Kossekechatko clung to the upturned canoe for many hours before they were able to right it and continue their journey. Despite the mishap they made a good voyage to Trinidad, landing at Chatham Bay on 7 August.

The following day they were taken before a magistrate and remanded in custody pending enquiries. Later they were sent to the prison to await the Governor's decision on their future.

The arrival of the three men created a sensation in Trinidad. Up to that time comparatively few *évadés* had managed to reach the colony and most of them had been sent back. This time the men appeared determined to make a stand against extradition to Guiana. Their case gained even more prominence when the Howard League for Penal Reform entered the scene on their behalf. The League, long active in prison circles in Britain, had recently extended their activities to the colonies and took immediate steps to block the expected extradition demand by the French Consul.

The three men put their case through the local and overseas Press and the Howard League retained counsel for them when they appeared before a magistrate to show good and just cause why they should not be returned to *le bagne* under an Anglo-French extradition agreement dating back to 1876. Despite their legal representation, however, the three men were remanded in prison pending the demand of the French authorities. Later they were allowed a stay of the order to enable them to appeal for a writ of *habeas corpus*.

The appeal came up before the Supreme Court of Trinidad. Counsel told the court that under the terms of the extradition agreement, clear evidence of a crime committed in the territory of either party must be shown. He submitted that this could not be done in the case of the *évadés* as they had committed no crime in French Guiana.

It was only a time-stalling legal technicality but it worked. Despite the Attorney General's assertion that the court could make a presumption that offences had been committed in French territory, the judge was doubtful.

But counsel had another trick up his sleeve. He pointed out that under the terms of the treaty an application for extradition had to be made within fourteen days of the arrest of the individuals concerned. The three men had reached Trinidad on 7 August, but the extradition application had not been received from the French Consul in Port of Spain until 24 October.

The whole affair presented interesting legal points and eventually the Supreme Court granted permission for the three men to appeal to the Privy Council in England. Meanwhile they were put into the care of the Salvation Army who lodged them in the hostel.

The wheels of law grind slowly and it was not until the end of July, 1931—356 days after their arrival in Trinidad—that the Privy Council ruling was given. After due and careful consideration the three law lords—Lord Atkin, Lord Thankerton and Lord Macmillan—ruled that the men should not be returned to *le bagne*.

There was then only the formality of a court appearance to listen to a police inspector tell the magistrates that the authorities did not wish to pursue the case and the men were free.

But by that time six other *évadés* had reached the island and there was agitation about them being allowed to remain in the colony. No steamship would take them to Europe or America because they were without passports and the British, however they might view the legal niceties of the case, were not disposed to hand out papers to every escaped convict who came their way.

The Salvation Army solved the problem by arranging for a seaworthy boat, adequately stocked with navigation equipment and food, to be given to Caullier, Retzenger and Kossekechatko and the six new arrivals. The nine men sailed out of Port of Spain harbour and headed due west in search of a country that might offer them refuge.[1]

It took some time for news of all this to reach *le bagne* but eventually an *évadé* named Mousset was captured in Venezuela and returned to Guiana. He had been one of the six men who had sailed with Caullier, Retzenger and Kossekechatko and knew all the details of the fight they had put up against extradition.

Perhaps the oddest of all the stories which I heard while I was at Montjoly was that of Leon Paquin, sent to *le bagne* in 1929 for killing at least five men in French Morocco. He told a strange story on his arrival. And when he departed mysteriously several years later those who remained behind felt that perhaps his lone and silent escape added the final chapter to his remarkable tale.

Paquin, a notorious thief and robber, was wanted by the police for several killings, all of them committed during the course of robberies. It took them nearly a year to run him to earth in Rabat and in a gun-battle with police and troops Paquin was wounded.

He was sent to a Roman Catholic hospital in Casablanca. There Paquin, the handsome, smooth-talking murderer, met Sister Therese Morin and they fell in love. Sister Therese was heart-broken when the courts sentenced Paquin to transportation and at their last meeting she made him a promise.

Her mother had left her a substantial sum of money which was held in a Paris bank. She promised Paquin that she would break her vows and go to Trinidad to make arrangements for an escape.

Paquin always had money in his *plan* and managed to bribe other convicts to do most of his work. He bought himself a comfortable and safe job in the Prison Administration and ruled his particular clique of convicts by his money and his reputation as a *fort-à-bras*.

[1] Details of the litigation in this case may be found in *The Times* of London Law Reports and in the files of the *Trinidad Guardian* in Port of Spain, Trinidad.—C.R.

And then one cool October night in 1937 Paquin left *le bagne*. There were no canoes missing; he could not have escaped into the jungle; it seemed unlikely that the ever-vigilant Dutch police would have missed him if he had crossed the Maroni.

But Leon Paquin was never heard of again.

Soon the tittle-tattle of the convicts began to embroider the story and it was believed that Sister Therese had indeed sent for her lover.

Just before I escaped to Venezuela I had met a man named Roger Vernon. He fled in 1927 and it was years before I heard what had happened to him. While I was at Montjoly I read some of it in a magazine.

On 24 January, 1936, a black police squad car raced to the scene of a grisly discovery under a roadside hedge near St. Albans, Hertfordshire. The body of a man had been found pushed into the undergrowth. He had a bullet wound in the stomach and had been dead for several hours. Immediately Scotland Yard's murder teams swung into action. From the man's clothing they decided that he was foreign and immediately his fingerprints and description were flashed to the police in every major city in Europe. Hours later France's *Sûreté Nationale* telephoned to say that the man was Max Kassel, alias Emil Allard, known to his friends as 'Max the Red'. Kassel, born in Riga, Poland, in 1879, had lived in Paris since 1901 and had been involved in drug-trafficking, murder, blackmail and white slaving. The Paris police were very interested to know that he was dead. They were even more interested in finding out who had killed him.

One of France's top detectives, Monsieur Magny, head of the *Sûreté Nationale*, happened to be in London for the funeral of King George V and Scotland Yard took full advantage of his presence. A few days after the discovery Magny flew back to France, collected a photographic album from the *Sûreté Nationale's* rogues' gallery and went to a Paris hospital where an alien lay ill. He was Max Kassel's brother.

The police forces of the two countries co-operated closely. Magny telephoned Scotland Yard with the names of several of Max's friends picked out of the photograph album by the brother. Scotland Yard detectives knew that one of the men, calling himself Lacroix, was in London. A flat belonging to a Frenchwoman, Suzanne Bertron, in Soho's Little Newport Street was raided but both Mme Bertron and the man they wanted had fled. A few hours later Inspectors Minter and Lander of Scotland Yard left for Paris. Three and a half hours after their arrival Lacroix and the woman were arrested in an hotel by French detectives. The man, calling himself Charles Lacroix, claimed that he was a French-Canadian and therefore a British subject. The woman, under her maiden name of Marguerite Ferrero, made the same claim. Lacroix was co-operative and offered to return to England with Minter and Lander. This intrigued the French police who could not understand why Lacroix should volunteer to be taken to England. They decided that he must have something to hide from the French police.

It took them eleven days to find out what it was.

Lacroix could not be budged from his story. He denied all knowledge of both Max Kassel and his death. But Suzanne Bertron was not so silent. When the couple appeared in court for a preliminary hearing, she told all she knew. She said that Kassel had visited her flat and told her that Lacroix owed him £25. Later she told Lacroix of the visit and he asked her to arrange for Max to be at the flat at six o'clock on 23 January. When Max arrived for the appointment Lacroix ordered her out of the flat and the next thing she saw was Kassel lying on the floor, dying. Later Lacroix removed the body.

Lacroix denied her whole story and told the court that he was a motor salesman working in Grafton Street. He said he went to the flat in Little Newport Street at eight o'clock on the evening that Kassel died, did not see 'Max the Red', dined and went to bed early. Day after day it went on. The police never stopped probing. Lacroix never faltered in his story. And then they had a stroke of luck. An old man from Fontenay-sous-Bois called on the *Sûreté Nationale* and told them he thought that Charles Lacroix was his son, Roger Vernon.

Now the French police knew why he had been anxious to co-operate with the British police and had offered to return voluntarily to London. Confronted by his father, Lacroix broke down and admitted that he was indeed Roger Vernon.

But he still denied all knowledge of Max Kassel or his death.

When Scotland Yard applied for an extradition warrant they met with strong resistance from the French authorities. The *Sûreté Nationale* had no intention of losing track of Roger Vernon. A judge denied the extradition order.

Later Vernon changed his story and confessed to the killing of Kassel, but claimed it was self-defence. He said that Kassel had tried to strangle him and that he had only shot him in order to save his own life.

In April, 1937, the French judge sent Roger Vernon to prison for ten years. Suzanne Bertron was released.

CHAPTER NINE

THE SALVATION ARMY officer in charge of Montjoly acted as a banker for we *libérés* by keeping the money we earned in a large safe in his office. One evening two men arrived from Cayenne with the plausible story that they had saved four thousand francs for their return passage but had heard that other *libérés* were plotting to steal it. The Captain took the money and locked it in a cash box because he had closed the safe for the night.

Later in the evening one of the *libéré* employees arrived at the Captain's house in a state of panic. The office had been broken into and ransacked. The officer went to the headquarters building and found everything in chaos. Papers were strewn everywhere, furniture was smashed and the cash box broken open and empty.

In the morning one of the *libérés* who had deposited his money the night before turned up to claim it. The other man, already boasting of the stupidity of the Army officer, was too drunk to come for his money. Knowing full-well that he had been taken in, the Captain had no choice but to pay out four thousand francs from the depleted funds and write the loss off to experience.

Some of the men broke up the furniture for fun. Others stole tools from the workshops, plants from the gardens, food from the restaurants and fuel from the stores to sell in town for rum money. They even sold the suits that the Army gave them.

Pay day was always a day of tension. The Montjoly officer, assisted by the *libéré* bookkeeper, Guillon, totted up what a man had earned, balanced it against what had been incurred in way of board and lodging, tobacco and stationery, and then paid out the remainder.

But sometimes the men disputed the accounting and caused trouble. Once the Lieutenant paying out was attacked and had his jaw broken by an enraged *libéré*.

The civil authorities were often hostile to the Army because they had befriended us. When an Arab murderer named Mansour, who had often given trouble on pay parades, got involved in a knife fight and then tried to kill the Lieutenant who intervened, it was the Army man who found himself hauled into the local court on a charge. The case got as far as the Court of Appeal before justice was done and the Lieutenant was discharged.

Other enemies of the Army, aiming at putting a stop to the plans to close *le bagne*, eventually persuaded even the *libéré* book-keeper to spy on the officers. Months later, thoroughly ashamed, the man left Montjoly and soon afterwards hanged himself in a fit of remorse.

Despite all the setbacks the Army pressed on.

The *libérés* who completed their *doublage* were technically free to return to France—if they could raise the two thousand francs needed for the passage. In practice it was terribly difficult for a man to support himself and save his fare money at the same time. So the Army instituted a scheme to aid any of the men who had completed or nearly completed this 'second sentence'.

To help them save the fare money these men received board and lodging free of charge; were entitled to use the amenities of the hostel; were given pocket money for sundry minor expenses, varying from one franc a day to fifty francs a month; and were provided with a coupon for forty francs at the end of each month which could be cashed at any time or held until twenty had been collected and could be exchanged for a third-class ticket home—the *Compagnie Générale Transatlantique* having offered reduced rates for returning *libérés*.

In February, 1936, Captain Pean was able to see part of his dream come true when the first shipload of repatriates sailed for France. He counted this a huge success, but it was only part of the programme and the fight to kill *le bagne* went on.

About this time I heard that my friend Henri De Bouyn had been recaptured. He had upset a cauldron of boiling water on himself while far back in the jungle and had been found quite delirious and near death by some Bush Negroes who put him into a canoe and paddled down the Maroni to the nearest hospital. It was the prison hospital. But De Bouyn was past caring. It was six months before he could walk again.

The Salvation Army officer at Montjoly persuaded the Administration that he was needed for plantation work and he rejoined us. But not for long. After a few weeks he escaped with a German convict and managed to get to British Guiana again. They sent him back. He did a stretch in the 'bear pits' on St. Joseph. Then he tried to escape again. He was caught and punished. He got away, this time to Venezuela, and was sent back. It happened again and again.

It all made me restless. The more I heard about escapes—and sometimes read about them in the French newspapers—the worse it got. I told myself that in eight years I could be repatriated, but it did not help. In eight years I might be dead—or crazy.

We talked a lot about Marie Bartet, the last surviving woman convict in *le bagne*. She was crazy.

Originally many hundreds of women had been sent to *le bagne*, the idea being that during the period that they were *libérés* they would marry men with the same prison status and settle down to raise families. This was part of the colonisation and population scheme for which the very existence of the penal settlements had been established.

The first thirty-four women were sent to *le bagne* in 1859 and within a year fifteen of them had died of tropical fevers. Another batch was sent out two years later. They married short-term convicts doing their *doublage* and six children were born to convict parents in 1862. After that groups of women convicts were sent to Guiana regularly. By 1869 there had been six shipments and they continued to arrive with every batch of male convicts until penal policy changed termporarily in 1888 and convicts—male and female—were sent to New Caledonia in the South Seas.

Marie Bartet was one of the last women to be sent to *le bagne* before the switch in policy. She spent fifty years in the colony and died a broken, crazy woman.

Marie was born in Marseilles in 1862 and at fifteen married a sailor from Bordeaux. He left her, and to support herself the girl stole food. Eventually she was caught and served a short sentence. On her release she stole again and was caught. It happened a third time and a fourth, and after the last conviction she was sent to Guiana as an incorrigible.

Marie was twenty-six years old when she arrived in Guiana in 1888 as a *relégué* and after twenty-one years she was allowed to marry an Arab *libéré* named Lakdar Ben Youcef who had been sent to Guiana for murder. The couple had two children, but both died young of fever and Lakdar died shortly after them. Marie withdrew into herself and refused to talk.

Only once in twenty-six years did she speak.

It was in 1912 when the authorities offered to repatriate her to France. Marie refused. All her memories were in Guiana. So were the graves of her husband and children. And she had been away from France for nearly a quarter of a century.

Marie grew older and more stooped in her little hut, and then even a little mad. She turned to God and was never seen without a Bible in her hand—even when transacting business and selling her vegetables.[1]

Finally I decided to go to live in Cayenne again. The Salvation Army officer begged me not to do so. He knew exactly what was going through my mind. But I disregarded his advice and left Montjoly for the squalor of the *libéré* settlement.

I soon found a vacant spot and put up a frame from which I hung sacks. Petrol tins covered part of the roof and kept me reasonably dry if it rained. I had no work. As in St. Laurent, there were few who would employ *libérés* without references, and who could get references? We scavenged in the dustbins, fighting for our share along with the vultures, crows, stray dogs

[1] Marie Bartet died in April, 1938, at the age of seventy-six. Just before she died in the arms of a nun she opened her eyes and said 'Thank God'. It was her second break of silence in twenty-six years.—C.R.

and cats. Often they got more than we did. I wanted to go back to Montjoly, but it would have meant admitting defeat so I held on for a little longer.

It was during my stay in Cayenne that I met Benjamin Ullmo, the only man, to my knowledge, who ever returned to *le bagne* of his own accord.

His story went back to before the First World War.

On 10 September, 1907, the French Naval Minister opened his mail and found among the normal business letters one that made him forget everything else that day and for the next few days. The letter, handwritten and bearing a Toulon postmark, informed him that the sender had photographic negatives of all the French Naval codes and signals, of her defence systems for the major ports, and of secret and top secret cyphers currently in use in the Navy. It added that the sender would sell the negatives to the Naval authorities for £7,500—and warned that if they did not buy them they would be sold to a foreign power, later identified as Germany. The Minister was instructed to put an advertisement in a Paris newspaper if he agreed to the deal and then await instructions.

He notified the *Sûreté Nationale* and put the advertisement in as instructed. Crack detective Pierre Sebille was assigned to the case and began to dicker with the blackmailer through the medium of newspaper advertisements. Eventually he got the price of the negatives reduced to £5,000.

Following the blackmailer's instruction Lieutenant Chardon of the French Admiralty took the night train from Paris on 30 September. Arriving at Toulon, he went to the General Post Office and asked for a letter addressed to 'Monsieur R. P. 349'. It told him to travel to Marseilles by a certain train and that in one of the washroom cupboards he would find a package containing the negatives. He was to put £5,000 in an envelope and leave it there. At Marseilles he was to wait in the station restaurant for forty-five minutes for the blackmailer to assure himself that the arrangement had been completed and then he was to go home.

Chardon tipped off his secret service colleagues to be on the train and then carried out his instructions to the full. He found eighteen negatives in a cupboard in one of the lavatories and left the money there as arranged.

But at Marseilles, while Chardon was in the restaurant, the proverbial innocent bystander blundered into the lavatory and was immediately arrested by the secret service men. He managed to identify himself as a French diplomat on holiday from Russia, but his accidental intrusion had ruined the plans. The authorities had the negatives, but they wanted the thief as well. And he wanted the money.

The following day the blackmailer started new arrangements with the French Admiralty, alleging that he had copies of the negatives.

On 22 October another agent of the *Sûreté Nationale* took a train to Toulon and booked in at an hotel as instructed. He later received a telephone call which told him to collect a letter at the Post Office and he found it contained instructions for him to take a taxi to a country village named Ollioules and then walk to a certain signpost and wait.

Sulzbach, the agent, did as he was instructed and after a few minutes a young man approached with a package in his hand. Sulzbach handed over the money without a word and watched as the man started to tuck it into an inside coat pocket.

As the man's eyes momentarily went to his pocket Sulzbach leapt forward and sent him crashing to the ground. After a short struggle he overpowered the man and handcuffed him. At the police station at Toulon the man was identified as Ensign Benjamin Ullmo of the French Navy.

At his court martial Ullmo confessed that he had got into financial difficulties through opium smoking and because of an expensive mistress known as 'La Belle Lison'. In desperation, for her tastes were highly priced, he had hoped to obtain money by selling negatives of French Naval secrets. While in temporary command of the gunboat *Carabine* he had opened the safe and photographed the documents. Ullmo added that he had tried to sell the negatives to a German agent he met in Paris, but the negotiations dragged on and he needed money quickly so he had tried to blackmail his own Government.

He was ignominiously dismissed from the Service and sentenced to life imprisonment for treason.

Ullmo was transported to Devil's Island, specially reserved for traitors and political prisoners, and left almost to his own devices. He was allowed to receive money and parcels from home and even reared chickens. The solitude nearly sent him mad. He began his sentence in 1908 and by 1921 it got too much for him. He tried to starve himself to death but was nursed by a convict named Deboe and by Dr. Rousseau, one of the prison doctors.

The Catholic priest, Father Fabré, looked up a law of 1873 relating to good conduct and after Ullmo had been on Devil's Island for fifteen years he was made a *libéré* and allowed to live on the mainland.

French newspaperman Albert Londres wrote about him and Ullmo got into correspondence with nursing sister Madeleine Poirier, the daughter of a distinguished French officer, who took up his case and worked for eleven years to have him released. Mainly due to her efforts Benjamin Ullmo, traitor, sailed for France twenty-six years after he had arrived on Devil's Island. And on the dock to meet him was Madeleine Poirier, describing herself as his 'fiancée'.

But Ullmo's freedom was short-lived.

On 10 January, 1935, Madeleine Poirier stood on the dock at Bordeaux for a second time and there were tears in her eyes. On the ship Benjamin Ullmo was giving interviews to Pressmen from all over France who had rushed to the port to talk to the man who was voluntarily going back to the hell of Guiana.

'What strikes a man, who for twenty-six years was out of touch with your civilisation, is the immeasurable stupidity of this humanity which thinks itself so superior,' Ullmo said. 'You confuse quantity and quality, size and greatness. Even in material things you have so lost a sense of values that you do not even realise how stupid and monotonous is your single passion to build larger, go faster—not to do better.

'I was deeply shocked on returning to Europe by the spiritual depression of the Old World,' he added. 'Humanity has lost all sense of reality. It is simply appalling to see the lowering of the moral level of your so-called civilisation.'[1]

Soon after meeting Ullmo, who at once promised to get me a job—as I afterwards learned he did every *libéré* he talked to—I was arrested for vagrancy. I should have gone back to Montjoly right then, but, hoping Ullmo would find something, I held on. Then came the second arrest.

It was not until I got into court that I found that there were two charges against me. I was found guilty on both counts—making a total of three charges of vagrancy.

I was numb when I heard the magistrate sentence me to become a *relégué*, confined for life to Guiana.

[1] I pieced together Ullmo's case from court records as well as from Etienne Artaud's story. Ullmo became a clerk in a warehouse in Cayenne and was still there in 1954.—C. R.

CHAPTER TEN

THE MAIN CAMP for the *relégués* was St. Jean-du-Maroni, a jungle work-camp twelve miles south of St. Laurent, connected to it by a small railway. There were no engines, for the carriages, like railcars, had seats under an awning at the front for two or three passengers. Behind them, without an awning, stood two convicts, the power that drove the railcars. Each man had a long pole which he used to propel the car along at little more than a walking pace.

That was how I got from St. Laurent to St. Jean.

At the camp sixteen hundred *relégués* worked in the forest from just after dawn until three in the afternoon cutting wood. A minimum requirement of one *stère*—about thirty-six cubic feet of wood—was demanded of us. If we finished it before time we were free to make our own way back to the barracks. If we could not finish it in time we were whipped and went without our supper—a bowl of soup and half a loaf of bread.

The death rate was fantastically high. About 350 new *relégués* arrived at the camp every year. But there were never more than sixteen hundred men there at any one time. It amounted to about one death a day—for there were few escapes from St. Jean.[1]

As chance would have it my arrival at St. Jean coincided with one of Leon La Durrell's last executions. In my condition of mind it was the last thing I could take not only because of the actual act of guillotining but because of the state of high excitement in which the convicts lived immediately before and after an execution.

In fact it all went off very quietly and smoothly. But it started

[1] George Seaton wrote: 'There were nearly 230 men in the consignment that arrived at St. Jean when I did. Within a year 140 of them were dead'—*Scars Are My Passport.*

the usual round of stories about executions and I heard the tale of Pellet who had been guillotined about five years earlier.

Obviously an educated man, Pellet had chosen silence and solitude as his weapon against the Administration, against the tyrannies of *le bagne*, and even against his fellow convicts. He had been in Guiana since 1901.

His only friend was a bank-clerk-turned-thief named Cusson. And even then the friendship was one sided. Cusson and Pellet worked together planting potatoes at St. Louis, the camp opposite the leper island.

The men there worked two to a potato mound, digging holes for the potatoes with machetes and then piling up the earth into little heaps. It was back-breaking, monotonous work. They returned to their huts at night completely exhausted. The best that could be said of it was that it was better than cutting wood in the jungle camps.

And then one day in the summer of 1930 Pellet's mind finally went.

He and Cusson were planting potatoes as usual when, suddenly and quite without warning, Pellet straightened up and swung his bush knife down at the bending Cusson. The man's skull split like a coconut and he crumpled over. Pellet wrenched his bush knife free of Cusson's head and went on digging as if nothing had happened.

For a moment the guards were stunned by the sheer suddenness of the brutality. Then they fell on Pellet with unsubdued savagery beating him into unconsciousness with clubs and whip before dragging him away to the punishment cells.

A *relégué* who protested that they would kill him with their beating was whipped and then manacled to a tree for three hours in the blazing sun. When freed he had to be carried to his barracks and within a week he was dead.

They took Pellet to *la veuve gaie* in a new cotton suit and strapped him to the board. He turned his head once and broke the virtual silence that had been his defence against *le bagne* for nearly thirty years.

He looked up at Leon La Durrell who stood shuffling his feet, and licking his lips.

'Bastard,' Pellet hissed out.

And then the knife dropped with a thud.

Shortly after the execution which coincided with my arrival at St. Jean it was decided that Leon La Durrell had earned a pardon.

He left *le bagne* wispy thin, bald, sick with malaria and prematurely old from the constant knife-edge life he had led in the Settlements. His only ambition was to return to Metz and take up his old job.

'There are plenty of advantages in being executioner,' he said on arrival in Paris. 'One is comparative freedom. You can't imagine what freedom means in that place. All the fifteen years I was there I received threats, and my life was not safe, but I was more a free man than any of the others.'[1]

They still talked of the mutiny at St. Jean when I arrived there. Few of the men who had lived through it had survived the rigours of life in the five years which followed. Those who had told every new arrival the story.

It had occurred in the summer of 1931. Its cause: butterflies.

One of the few extra ways of making money that the Administration allowed the *relégués* was the catching and selling of the magnificent Guiana butterflies to tourists in Cayenne or St. Laurent and to the Salvation Army. The five francs earned for each specimen was equal to about seventeen days' pay and *relégués* guarded this privilege jealously.

In the summer of 1931 a *transporté* named Chalot Cutureot escaped from the Camp des Malagaches and ran riot in the jungle. Lone *relégués* from St. Jean, out catching butterflies, were barbarously murdered for their trophies and then hacked open for their *plans*. The authorities scoured the surrounding country for Cutureot but failed to find him and eventually St.

[1] Quoted from *Paris-Soir*. La Durrell was pardoned in 1937. A year later he was found with a knife in his back in a Paris street. Vengeance, perhaps, from some *évadé* on the run? The crime was never solved.—C. R.

Jean's Commandant issued an order that the collection of butterflies was to be discontinued.

The *relégués* were outraged. The sole privilege they enjoyed was being taken from them. The money they were able to spend on extra food—or escaping—was being cut off.

A leading *fort-à-bras* organised a sit-down strike and the convicts refused to leave their huts for two days. On the morning of the third day the Senegalese troops were brought down from St. Laurent. They charged in among the huts and more than fifty *relégués* were bayoneted to death.

I had barely settled in before I was sent to St. Louis Camp, opposite the leper island in the Maroni. There I dug potatoes until it was discovered that I was good at carpentry. At first I formed part of a work party that was repairing the barracks. Then I was given an individual assignment: to go and reshingle the roofs of the lepers' huts.

An island of men, half-men and men who were no longer human—that was the leper island of St. Louis. When they sent me to work there I felt that I had been sentenced to death. New Camp was a haven compared with that place. It would have been preferable to have gone to work in the civilian leper camp at Acaranouay. At least they were kept clean and disinfectant was used. I was taken over by launch every morning and collected every evening. The job lasted a week and I never worked so quickly in all my days in *le bagne*. For once I was eager to finish a job. In fact, I couldn't finish soon enough to suit me.

At various times the leper island has been used for escapes. At other times it was the hide-out for *évadés* waiting until the heat was off to cross the Maroni and try their luck in the dense jungle of Dutch Guiana.

When I first went there I felt sick. The first leper I saw was probably the worst. But for the first day each one looked more terrible than the last. I fell asleep that night and saw those terribly deformed men dragging themselves around the island. Men with no ears; men with half their faces eaten away; men with a round red hole where an eye should have been; men with one leg gone;

with both legs gone; with no fingers; with no arms. Terrible creatures who would just grunt when they saw you, but who you knew resented you for being whole.

The lepers had a boat which was sunk during the day and raised at night for trips to the Chinese section of St. Laurent where they gambled and drank *tafia* until dawn and then paddled back to the island. Sometimes a leper would be found dead drunk in the street, but he was never punished. When he sobered up he was told to go back to the island. For punishment meant men touching him and things touching him. It meant cells—and lepers were not wanted in cells.

Every morning the prison boat put out from the mainland camp of St. Louis and called at the island. No leper was allowed to stand on the beach when the launch approached and the trusty at the bows just dumped the bag containing the day's food on the shore and then the boat went back to St. Louis Camp. How the lepers distributed the food was their affair—the Administration had provided food and that was enough.

Once a month a trusty named Rainouart, who was the lepers' medical orderly, visited the island to give them injections of chaulmoogra oil, which does not cure leprosy but sometimes arrests its growth.

Rainouart himself was not a leper. He had been in *le bagne* for fifteen years before becoming the orderly for the island and it was seven years before he himself contracted the disease and died.

The job of orderly gave him an opportunity for graft. He sold what he could. Tinned milk, clothing, food-stuffs of any kind, disinfectant, medical supplies like iodine and chaulmoogra oil; everything, in fact, had its price in *le bagne*. The doctors who came out from France seldom visited the island more than once. They arrived keen and new, saw the impossible task ahead of them—and left it to the orderly.

Men with the white of their facial bone showing through decayed flesh, mingled with the legless, the armless, the blind and the mad. Nobody was whole on St. Louis. Each one was a dreadful parody of humanity in a tropical paradise island with breadfruit and mango trees reaching down to the water's edge.

Convicts and lepers often traded. *Libérés* would paddle to the island to buy the eggs laid by the lepers' hens. These could be re-sold at a profit in St. Laurent. Other *libérés*, smuggling flour from Albina, used St. Louis as a holding base for the merchandise, collecting it when they wanted it. Lepers went to St. Laurent to buy *tafia*. Or *libérés* came to them to sell it.

From time to time *fort-à-bras* took refuge on the island. Sometimes it was a preliminary to an escape bid. Sometimes it was to escape from the work and discipline of the camps. A few came silently at night and kept the location of their canoes secret in case they should ever want to leave in a hurry. A few bribed convicts working in the Administration to mark them down as lepers.

The Bush Negroes would often help an *évadé* to escape. If he were sick they would care for him. But this was not always true, for some returned them for the few francs that the Administration paid for escapers.

A leper, on the other hand, could never expect help. To protect themselves from disease the Negroes killed them automatically. One man was halfway to Paramaribo before he met anyone. The Bush Negroes killed him as soon as they saw that he was a leper. Another, a mad German leper named Joseph Pistar, a former soldier in the Foreign Legion, escaped in 1938 after twelve years in *le bagne*. He was never heard of again so the authorities believed that either the Bush Negroes or the Indians had got to him before he reached civilisation.

Life for a guard's house-boy was either very soft or very hard. There was no in-between stage. Single guards made applications for the best-looking of the new arrivals and inducted them into *le bagne* as *mômes*. Married guards and their wives used their house-boys as cooks, chamber maids, and general lackeys. It was cheaper to have a house-boy from among the convicts than to have to pay a local Guianese.

One house-boy fell in love with the guard's wife and she with him. The husband neglected his wife and had affairs with the wives of other guards. She turned to the convict for sympathy. He lived in the camp, careful not to infringe the rules or anger the guard for whom he worked. By day he was in the house and he and the guard's wife were lovers. The husband never discovered, as he seldom spent much time at home anyway.

And then the house-boy contracted leprosy. He told no one in the camp. But he told his mistress. She said it did not matter. Life to her was nothing without the house-boy. In time she also contracted leprosy.

When the husband discovered the lovers one day the wife shielded her house-boy and told the husband that they were both lepers. She begged him to say nothing about it and told him that she could not live without her lover.

The following day the house-boy did not report for duty. The guard had betrayed him and he was on his way to St. Louis island. His wife was to be sent to the civilian leper camp at Acaranouay, but a few days before she was to go she took her husband's gun and blew her brains out.

When Paul Dubois, a *fort-à-bras*, discovered that he had leprosy he was lying in the hospital on Isle Royale recovering from a severe bout of tropical fever brought on in the 'bear pits' of St. Joseph. Dubois had been in Guiana for nearly twenty years and had spent fifteen of them on the islands doing additional sentences for escape bids.

The medical orderly came from the same village as Dubois and they had served together in the same regiment during the First World War. Because of this the *fort-à-bras* received special treatment and extra care, recovering from a fever that would have killed most other convicts.

A few days before he was due to be discharged the doctor noticed a rash on his hand and without saying anything made the standard tests for leprosy. They were positive. The doctor told the orderly that Dubois would be sent to St. Louis when he was discharged.

Dubois, when he got over his first shock, went to the doctor and begged him to release him from the hospital for a week. He had an escape already planned, the canoe was ready, all he wanted was a chance. He promised that if he were still on Royale at the end of a week they could send him to St. Louis.

The doctor refused.

Dubois pleaded to be set free for two days. He appealed to the doctor as a fellow military man. Again he met blank refusal and mounting anger.

Dubois went back to the ward a broken man. Then he decided to have one last try with the doctor. A few minutes later he joined his orderly friend in the lavatory and told him that he had beaten out the doctor's brains.

The orderly knew that there would be a guillotining for this. He gave Dubois a powerful sedative and when the doctor's body was found Dubois was sound asleep and could not be awakened. The ward was turned upside down by the guards and then someone remembered seeing Dubois going to the doctor's office. They examined his clothes and found blood on them.

The orderly knew that he must work fast to be of any help to his boyhood friend. Quickly he mixed a draught of poison in the dispensary and then forced it down Dubois' throat while he lay unconscious. A few minutes later two guards arrived, detailed to sit by Dubois' bed until he regained consciousness. Of course, he never did. The orderly had done his job well. He had saved his friend from either St. Louis island or the guillotine. Where he had gone no one from *le bagne* could touch him.

Suspicion rested on the orderly but nothing could be proved. Dubois might have been able to poison himself while the doctor lay dead in his office and the orderly was at the other end of the ward.

Then there was Gerardin who used leprosy as a way out of *le bagne* only to have the grisly disease catch up with him later.

Gerardin spent ten years in Guiana before he thought of a plan to get away. His chance came when he was at the dreaded Camp Charvin for punishment work. The convicts were shackled in pairs at night and Gerardin's chain-mate developed leprosy.

There was no doubt that it was genuine and he was sent to St. Louis. And in this Gerardin saw his chance.

He cut off some fingers and half an ear. The pain was excruciating, but he felt that the result was worth it. A local plant gave a juice which prevented the wounds from bleeding and soon he really looked the part. The doctors did not think even the tests necessary. It was leprosy without a doubt. Gerardin was sent to St. Louis.

The very first night he raised the dugout which the lepers used for their nocturnal visits to St. Laurent and paddled down the river. He bought supplies in the town and then put out to sea. It took him ten days to reach Paramaribo and from there he took a ship to Brazil, bumming round the coastal towns for a while before going to São Paulo.

Then came the ironical twist. One day after several months in São Paulo he noticed that a tattoo mark on his arm had swollen a little. He pricked it with a pin but there was no pain. He was certain that it was an insect bite, but a nagging fear played on his mind. Eventually he went to a doctor just to make sure. The doctor diagnosed leprosy.

The authorities learned that he had escaped from *le bagne*. And the French Consul was told. It was his problem to get Gerardin back there. But no ship would take him. No prison in Brazil would accept him either. There was only one thing to do. The Brazilians sent him to the leper colony at Piratipingui, and to keep him away from the other lepers—they never forgot that he was a criminal—they built a special little hut for him and surrounded it with barbed wire. Gerardin's leprosy was of a mild kind. His every need was catered to. He grew flowers around his hut. He was as happy as he could ever be with the disease.

After all, he could never be sent back to *le bagne*.

These were the kind of stories you heard while at St. Louis Camp and I was glad to be sent back to St. Jean after a while.

CHAPTER ELEVEN

A MURDERER NAMED SOUSTELLE who had, like me, been found guilty of vagrancy during his period of *doublage*, arrived at St. Jean early in 1939. He brought us the latest news of the Salvation Army and of their repatriation of *libérés*. It broke my heart to think that if I had not been made a *relégué* I would have been only five years off repatriation myself.

The first repatriation from *le bagne* had been allowed in February, 1936, and the mail boat *Flandre* sailed for St. Nazaire with sixty-seven *libérés* whose fares and been paid by the Salvation Army. They picked up three *évadés* in Venezuela and Captain Pean, who was the officer in charge, took them with the party rather than send them back to Guiana. There were men from several countries in that party. I had watched them assemble at Montjoly to go down to Cayenne. They included Frenchmen, a Senegalese, a Syrian, an Indo-Chinese who returned with his two-year-old son, and about thirty Arabs. They wore turbans, colonial sun-helmets and battered caps and their few belongings were bundled into sacks. The Indo-Chinese had a deck-chair as his sole souvenir of twelve years in Guiana. Three of the men were from St. Nazaire. One had been away ten years, another fourteen, the third eighteen. They were disembarked and the rest of the party, joined by Captain Pean, went on to Le Havre. From there they went to Paris and later thirty-one of the men left from the Gare de Lyon for various destinations. Another eighteen went to Marseilles. Others dispersed in their respective directions. The Arabs left Marseilles by sea for Oran, Tunis and Algiers, to be met by the Salvation Army and taken to their villages. The Senegalese sailed for Dakar and later wrote to Pean expressing his gratitude.

That was the first party. Others followed. Month after month ragged men arrived from *le bagne* to be re-united with wives, parents, brothers, sisters and friends they had not seen for half a lifetime. Altogether eight hundred *libérés* went home before the war came.

I knew that we would be having a different type of prisoner in *le bagne* after the reforms which the Salvation Army had been pressing for became law. France had not dared to end *le bagne* in one swoop. All murderers already there would remain to finish their sentences. Thieves with several convictions would still be sent out as *relégués*. But on 22 November, 1938, *La Martinière*, left Ile de Ré with what was to be the last boatload of convicts to be transported. We could not, of course, know that then and I watched the *relégués* among them arriving at St. Jean just as thousands had arrived before.

* * *

In France support for the suppression of the penal colony was under way. On 3 September, 1936, the Keeper of the State Seals, who was also a member of the *Comité d'Honneur*, had said in an interview with *Paris-Soir*: 'I have always been in favour of the suppression of *le bagne*, and have been dealing with the question for a long time.'

The two Government Ministries involved in the administration of *le bagne*—Colonies and Justice—were also headed by men interested in seeing an end of the penal colony. The Keeper of the State Seals set up an inter-ministerial commission for the suppression of the colony and within six months they placed a 'Bill for the Abolishment of the Penal Settlement' before the Chamber of Deputies.

Towards the end of 1937 the Salvation Army was able to hold a mass rally under the auspices of the *Comité d'Honneur* at which many influential government men spoke in favour of closing French Guiana as a penal settlement for ever.

The Minister of Justice said: 'One can sentence a criminal to life imprisonment. The law allows the passing of the death sentence. But our hearts, our innermost feelings, our diverse beliefs, our Christianity in particular, forbid us to sentence a man to descend lower than he actually is.'

Paul Matter, President of the Court of Appeal, said: 'Is it possible by gentle reforms to change this system which is the object of such just and vehement criticism? Have regulations and modifications been able to transform *le bagne*, not into a paradise but, let us say, into a purgatory? I speak about this question with nearly fifty years' service as a magistrate. After all I have seen and read, I say *le bagne* must be abolished.'

But even the efforts of the most influential men in France failed to get *le bagne* closed down. The food which was sent to the colony was improved but that was all. And even the food had little effect on the inmates. Graft had always kept *le bagne* moving at a smooth and profitable pace for a few and they received by far the greater advantages from any changes.

Again time dragged by. Convicts still escaped from *le bagne*. The Salvation Army still pressed for closure of the Settlements.

And then, on 17 June, 1938, the President of the Republic sent a report to the Prime Minister.

It read: 'For many years, in spite of the improvements carried out in the living conditions of transported criminals, severe criticisms have been made concerning *le bagne* in Guiana. In point of fact, *le bagne* does not appear to have any deterrent effect upon the criminals themselves and does not provide them with any means of moral reformation or of rehabilitation. From another point of view, the presence in the only French colonial possession in America of a penal transport establishment is not good for the prestige of France in that continent. Escaped prisoners are scattered through Brazil, Venezuela and Colombia, where they form unhealthy and dangerous groups, surrounded by a suspicion that reacts on our countrymen . . .

'In addition, in order to have any moral value, punishment should subject the prisoner to some regular work. Actually, experience shows that penal labour cannot, in the climate of Guiana, constitute a labour force for colonisation purposes. It would therefore seem vain to anticipate any alteration in the convicts themselves as a result of their work in the penitentiary . . . *le bagne* should disappear by extinction and Guiana will then be able to adopt itself progressively to a new economy.'

But despite the President's desire to close *le bagne* he was unable to repatriate convicts already there and the measures the Prime Minister was asked to sign alleviated the penal code, but did not change it sufficiently to ensure the closure of the penal settlement. Murderers were to remain in *le bagne* and thieves—*relégués*—would still be sent there. *La Martinière* would still ply her sinister way across the Atlantic.

But other factors were combining to force an end to *le bagne*. The sailing from St. Martin de Ré on 22 November, 1938, was destined to be the last because the Second World War would come before another sailing and so disrupt the world's steamship transportation that another shipment would be impossible.[1]

* * *

At Christmas, 1939, we learned that France was at war.

A *libéré* from Cayenne who had been hunting butterflies came secretly into camp at night and gave us the news. He also told us that *La Martinière* had been stripped of her steam hoses and machine guns and turned into a pontoon to be used at the mouth of the River Loire.

In *le bagne* life went on pretty much as usual. At first there was a burst of patriotism because France, our France which had broken our bodies and twisted our minds, was at war. But this soon wore off.

In January, 1940, I was sent to Isle St. Joseph, not for punishment but as part of a working party who were constructing new wooden barracks on the island. It had been decided that most of the convicts in the mainland camps would be transferred to St. Joseph and Royale and accommodation was required for them.

A few days after my arrival the whole place was buzzing with

[1] Etienne Artaud did not know the background to the closure of *le bagne* and I have filled it in from contemporary legal records and from *Conquest of Devil's Island* by Captain Charles Pean.—C.R.

the news that George Bonfils, the island executioner, had been captured trying to escape. Surprised by a guard while digging up a canoe he had hidden, Bonfils killed him but was captured by a second guard who caught him launching the boat.

A killer named Serge Corbière was nominated by the Administrator to replace Bonfils—and, of course, to execute him.

Corbière, an incorrigible escaper, was a well-known character in the penal colony. He had been sent to *le bagne* in 1933 and had done several stretches in the 'bear pits' for unsuccessful escapes and had only been captured a matter of weeks before following a bid which had ended in the deaths of his six companions. He had been found in the jungle quite mad and was suspected of cannibalism. He had regained his sanity in the St. Laurent hospital and the Administrator, thinking to put him in a position where he would not be able to escape, made him the island executioner in place of Bonfils.

Unknown to the authorities, Bonfils had buried a second boat and he told Corbière about it. On 10 February, 1940, the new executioner pulled the lever which sent the weighted knife crashing down to slice off Bonfils's head. The guards left him to clear up the mess and put the body into a shroud for burial at sea. Corbière, remembering the Count of Monte Cristo, put Bonfils's head and body in a cupboard and rolled himself into the shroud. When the guards returned they carried the 'body' to the boat, took it out to sea and tossed it over. Corbière surfaced and swam to the shore where he made his way to Bonfils's boat and headed for Brazil. He was picked up by a coastguard cutter of the Brazilian Navy and given asylum until he eventually escaped to France.[1]

The executioner who had preceded Bonfils had been a macabre humorist named Hespel. Tattooed on his chest were the words 'Live who can! Die who must!'

[1] In March, 1941, Corbière reached France and joined the Underground movement—the Maquis. In 1945 he surrendered to the authorities but, instead of being pardoned, he was jailed. Maquis friends broke him out of jail and got him out of the country. He now lives in the old French colony of San Raphael, in the state of Veracruz, in the Republic of Mexico.—C.R.

After completing the building of the new barrack blocks on St. Joseph I was returned to St. Jean. There were fewer men there now and the work was much harder. Men who had survived years in *le bagne* just gave up and died. Others ran into the bush and hanged themselves. Many paddled across the Maroni on rafts to seek asylum in Dutch or British Guiana and to try to join the Free French Forces. Still others paddled northwards to Trinidad and the other islands of the West Indies.[1]

Then came the news of the fall of France.

The Commandant mustered us and told us that French Guiana must remain loyal to Marshal Pétain's Vichy Government. Simultaneously came the news that both General de Gaulle and the Vichy Administration were sending Governors to the colony. The Vichy man arrived first and soon the rumours ran wild that German submarines were being refuelled along the coast. The Americans began to take an interest. So did the British. Neither of them wanted a secure German refuelling base in the Western Hemisphere—particularly one so close to the all-important Caribbean and the South Atlantic.

And then new convicts began to arrive from Guadeloupe and Martinique, the French islands in the Eastern Caribbean. These were political prisoners in every sense of the word. Both islands had turned to the Vichy Government and most of the new arrivals were loyalists who had been caught inciting men to flee to the British islands and go from there to fight for de Gaulle.

Among the early arrivals were a Frenchman, Herman Gachette, and a Russian named Romnich who had been arrested in Martinique for aiding French sailors to escape to the British island of St. Lucia. Within a week of their arrival they had made a raft out of a door, given it buoyancy with coconut fibre and paddled away from *le bagne*.

[1] In mid-1940 there were thirty *évadés* in Puerto Rico waiting to be sent to England to enlist in the Free French Forces. The following year there were 176 men in Trinidad waiting for a ship to take them to Britain. Dutch Guiana had supplied transport to Trinidad for 130 of them who had reached Albina or Paramaribo. British Guiana had forwarded forty-six who turned up in Georgetown.—C.R.

Cut off from Europe, the import of food to *le bagne* was strangled. Rations dropped to virtual starvation point. A mug of coffee, a small tin of corned beef between four men, a handful of rice, a bowl of thin soup and 250 grammes of bread was our day's ration. And then we were ordered to cut an extra half-*stère* of wood a day. Later this was again raised and we toiled from dawn to dusk to cut two *stères* a day.

The two New Camps, the one for *transportés* and the other for *relégués*, where the sick and maimed were sent to die, were activated. Men on the verge of death were given axes and sent into the jungle to cut wood. Then the population of St. Jean was slashed by half. Legally it was forbidden to mix *transportés* and *relégués*, but these were times of war and half of the St. Jean men were sent to St. Laurent.

I was one of those left at St. Jean to cut wood on starvation rations. In the year since the beginning of the war about six hundred men had died in the camp.

Early in 1941 the men who poled the rail-cars down from St. Laurent to St. Jean arrived in a state of great excitement with news of a mass escape.

Captain Claude Chandron, a veteran of World War One, had been recruiting for the Free French. He was a prominent man in the colony, a fine old soldier who had won the Croix de Guerre in the war and had then come to Guiana to start a banana plantation up the Sinamary River.

The Vichy Governor had refused to allow Chandron to recruit in the colony. He also refused to allow the Captain to take the able-bodied men and the Senegalese troops into Dutch Guiana in the hope of getting transport to America or Britain. So Chandron took the law into his own hands. In St. Laurent he began a secret recruiting drive among the convicts. Soon he had three hundred men ready to march with him. His army, drawn from the worst of France's criminals, included forgers, murderers, rapists, bank robbers, blackmailers and thieves. But all swore to follow the Captain. They joined for different reasons: some from genuine desire to fight for the country which had disowned them, others because they thought that enlistment might offer an opportunity for desertion in war-torn Europe. A few hoped that volunteer war service would earn them pardons later.

Chandron went to Paramaribo, arranged a deal with the Dutch, and one night in February, 1941, a fleet of canoes and dugouts crossed the Maroni from the Dutch side of the river. They returned with 130 *libérés*. Chandron sent money to *transportés* and *relégués* to follow later if they could. His army was transferred to Paramaribo by sea and eventually they joined the Free French and saw service in Brazzaville in French Equatorial Africa.

A month after the army had left about 170 *transportés* and *relégués* tried to follow suit. Most of them were arrested and sentenced to five years in the St. Joseph 'bear pits' as traitors.

I wished that I had been at St. Laurent at the time because Chandron's 'army' had offered the best opportunity to escape from *le bagne* for a long time. Soon afterwards the number of the men at St. Jean was reduced again and I was among those sent to St. Laurent, but it was too late then.

There was a constant excitement at the camp because loyalist prisoners were arriving in chains from the French West Indian islands. They were all bound for the 'bear pits' of St. Joseph. They came in ones and twos, they came in tens and twenties. Everywhere the Vichy Administrations were fighting to hold down the de Gaullists who agitated in their midst. French civil servants from Cayenne accused of writing de Gaulle propaganda leaflets were joined by Negro journalists from Martinique who had rallied people to escape to the British islands, and coloured merchants from Guadeloupe who had allowed their trading vessels to carry men to Barbados and the Leeward Islands.

The Salvation Army suffered badly during these lean years in *le bagne*. In 1941 the area headquarters in Jamaica assumed financial responsibility for the *Bureau de Bagne* but wartime conditions forced the Army to abandon their beloved Montjoly. The Vichy Governor visited his displeasure on them and in

February, 1942, made the officer-in-charge an official scapegoat, ordering him out of the colony as 'dangerous to the safety of the State'. It was alleged that he had incited *libérés* to flee to Dutch Guiana to join the Free French. He was sent to Martinique with his wife and interned.

The presence of the Salvation Army officers had been a small but valued asset to us. They had been a sort of watch dog on the Administration and had spent a lot of their time protesting about the treatment being meted out to prisoners. After the senior officer left the whole place went mad. We heard that they were flogging men to death every day at Kourou, Charvin and St. Jean, and things were not much better at St. Laurent. Men were dying of exhaustion and malnutrition and they did not bother to bury them behind The Bamboos any more. They were just put into crates and tipped into the Maroni.

We were forced to cut two *stères* of wood a day. Even the *fort-à-bras* had to work. And their *mômes*.

My friend of Cayenne and Montjoly days, Henri De Bouyn, succeeded in escaping again in 1942 and reached Trinidad where there were thirteen other *évadés* already. The local police gave them a boat and they pushed on northwards through the islands. I heard this from a loyalist journalist who was sent to *le bagne* from Martinique but I never knew what happened to them.[1]

In 1943 Jean Rapenne, the Vichy Governor, fled to Brazil after the civilian population of Cayenne rioted in the streets over the reported refuelling of German U-boats. The colony was the first to break away from the Vichy Government in France.

[1] Eight of the men with De Bouyn were Europeans of non-French origin. Only six had French nationality. They stopped at several islands on their voyage up the Eastern Caribbean chain of islands which they hoped would eventually get them to the United States. And at each island a man found sanctuary in the consul of his native land. They sailed west from Antigua to the Dominican Republic and there the seventh of the non-Frenchmen was allowed to stay. De Bouyn pushed on with two French Moroccans and three French Indo-Chinese. They were wrecked near Acklins Island in the Bahamas and De Bouyn still lives there, a highly respected sculptor and the man who designed and executed the memorial to the Bahamians who died while flying with the Royal Air Force in the war.—C.R.

But by that time the convict population of *le bagne* had been reduced by half.[1]

[1] Convict George Seaton wrote later: 'I was able to piece together a picture of *le bagne* after the closing of St. Jean. The 6,000 *condamnés* and *relégués* had been reduced by half. Of the 1,600 *relégués* who had been at St. Jean only 290 remained alive. The 200 lepers of St. Louis Island now numbered 80. The 400 incurables of New Camp had risen to 700—the New Camp for *transporté* incurables had been closed and the convicts were bundled in with the *relégués*. The 3,000 convicts who had been scattered among the Isles of Salvation and the mainland were now 1,500 strong and were all at St. Laurent, with the exception of a few *assignés* at Cayenne. The 800 *libérés* and *popottes* of 1940 had been halved. There were no *concessionaires* Approximately 3,000 men had died in *le bagne* in two and a half years since the fall of France.'—*Scars Are My Passport.*

CHAPTER TWELVE

EARLY IN MARCH, 1945, I could take *le bagne* no longer. So I escaped. It was not very difficult. The whole structure of the place had broken down. Nobody knew where anybody was —nobody really cared. I just walked off into the jungle. Days later friendly Bush Negroes took me to their village and fed me. They were heading up the Maroni in canoes and I asked to go with them. I went far into the interior to their village, possibly deeper into the unexplored forests than any white man had ever been.

In the foothills of the Tumac Humac Mountains we met a strange and silent Indian. The Bush Negroes spoke several dialects, but they could not understand the man. He had a little bag with him and showed me some small nuggets of gold. By signs he made us understand that he came from Brazil and that he knew where other white men were finding gold. They could, I knew, only be *évadés*.

I decided to go with him and said good-bye to the Bush Negroes. It took us a week, following narrow jungle paths ever southward towards the Equator, and then one noon we walked into a settlement of sorts which was the gold camp the Indian had spoken about. Before I could even thank him he was gone and I was alone in a strange and possibly hostile place.

But I need not have worried.

One of the first men I met in the camp was an *évadé* named Pierre Guillon who had escaped from *le bagne* with the famous Armand Spilers in 1932. I had never met Spilers but had read, while at Montjoly, of his fantastic escapes not only from Guiana but from French prisons as well.

He was called 'King of the Gaolbreakers' and had often boasted that there was no gaol in the world which could hold him for long. He was a burglar by profession and had operated in several countries. In 1925 the Belgian police had captured him and he was given a sentence in the security-plus gaol at Loos.

It did not take him long to escape. A few weeks after he began his sentence he grabbed a warder through the bars of his cell, relieved him of his keys, gun and uniform and locked him up. Then, bidding a cheerful good-morning to everyone he met, he calmly walked out of the gaol and caught a bus to the nearest railway station.

The following year he was in France at the head of a burglary syndicate which opened up a crime wave that kept the Paris police on their toes for several months until Spilers was caught on the job and gaoled. A judge sentenced him to fifteen years in Guiana and he sailed on *La Martinière* at the end of the year. Even *le bagne* held no terrors for Spilers. They put him in the escape-proof 'bear pits' on St. Joseph just to give him a taste of the maximum security cells that could be awarded to troublesome prisoners. He came out of the cells determined on one thing: he was not going to be in Guiana for long. In 1929 he left by night in a dugout and crossed the Maroni. Almost at once he ran into Dutch border guards and was sent back. The warders smiled when he arrived at St. Joseph again, this time for two years of punishment. In 1931 he was returned to the mainland. The fanatical escaper who would take any chance to flee his prison was dead inside him. In his place was a shrewd and crafty schemer, determined to get away at all costs and determined to have a foolproof escape plan before risking the attempt.

The following year he was ready. This time Spilers chose five men to go with him. One of them was Guillon. All were experienced convicts and men who had made escape bids before. They all had a taste of the 'bear pits' and knew what failure would mean. They put to sea in a dugout with a flimsy sail and steered east along the coast of Brazil. The blazing sun burned into their backs from shortly after dawn until sunset. Their lips cracked and their skin reddened and peeled off. One man went mad and flung himself into the sea. Soon afterwards another, not satisfied with the small ration of water the convicts allowed themselves, began drinking sea water. Soon he, too, went mad and leapt overboard. After nearly two weeks at sea the four remaining convicts staggered ashore. One of them died soon after and was left to rot while the other three, led by Spilers, struck inland in the hope of finding an Indian or Bush Negro village.

They lived on berries, roots and small lizards. Sometimes they trapped jungle rats or parrots. Most of the time they starved. They grew weaker and weaker. Tempers grew thin. And then one night Spilers' two companions quarrelled and Guillon stuck his knife in the other's throat. The men had not eaten for three days and had little chance of trapping anything in their weakened state. There seemed nothing else to do except begin on their dead companion.

Months later they staggered into a little gold camp far back in the interior of Brazil and joined the ragged band of prospectors who were panning a fast-running stream for dust and a few nuggets. They were lucky. A few days after they had started Spilers trapped a nugget in their pan and from then on they never looked back. Dust, nuggets, quartz. They found them all. Within weeks they were comparatively rich. They had regained their strength and their money enabled them to buy the best of supplies from the Chinese trader who supplied the gold camp.

Then Guillon was badly injured in a knife fight with another prospector who left him for dead and stole his poke of gold dust and nuggets. Guillon told Spilers to get out while he still could and the escape-king left.

He had panned enough gold to make him moderately wealthy and from the camp he went to Caracas where he bought a passport and the necessary documents from a forger and sailed for France as 'Monsieur Dupuis'.

In Paris Spilers bought a small restaurant and was re-united with his wife and daughter. He tried to go straight but soon he craved excitement. He was jumpy and nervous when there were strangers about. When he was alone with his wife he was irritable.

Early in 1936, while out walking his dog a man on a bicycle ran into it and a fight between the man and Spilers ensued. Eventually the convict pulled a revolver on the man and at the same moment a gendarme arrived. Spilers was taken to police headquarters and his fingerprints checked.

The police took him to the fortress of La Santé, the strongest prison in Paris, and locked him away pending removal to St. Martin-de-Ré and a return trip to *le bagne*. But Spilers was not without contacts. One smuggled him a file. Another arranged for a rope to be thrown over the prison wall. A third held a fast car in readiness for the getaway.

On 20 March, 1936, Spilers waited until the guard had made his final check on the cells and then got off his bunk. He put a dummy in the bed, stuck his nightcap on its 'head' and then set to work on the bars.

An hour later a bar came free and Spilers wriggled through the gap and dropped twelve feet to the courtyard below. He sprinted across the yard, grabbed the rope that his accomplice had thrown over the thirty-foot high wall, and scaled it. Outside he dropped to the ground and ran to the getaway car. His escape was not discovered until the next morning when a warder put his hand on Spilers' 'shoulder' and found that it was a dummy. The alarm was sounded and La Santé was surrounded. But it was too late. Spilers was a hundred miles away. The police found where he had scaled the wall. They found marks on a tree which the accomplice had climbed in order to throw the rope over the wall. They found tyre tracks on the road. And that was all.

The escape from the so-called 'escape-proof' prison caused an immediate sensation. Only once in the history of La Santé had a man escaped from it, and that was not by filing his way out. The first escaper was the Royalist Léon Doudet who was released by the authorities after a fake telephone call instructing the Governor to turn him loose.

Some of the most dangerous men in France were held in La Santé and immediately security precautions were trebled.

Another *évadé* was in the prison at the time awaiting trial. He was Roger Vernon, wanted by the French police for an escape from Guiana and by Scotland Yard for the Soho murder of 'Max the Red' Kassel, white slaver. Immediately it was claimed that a secret criminal organisation was helping convicts to escape from Guiana and then aiding them if they were recaptured in France.

Meanwhile an extensive hunt was on for Armand Spilers but it was not until nearly a fortnight later that the police learned of his whereabouts. He had crossed the Franco-Spanish border and then written to his wife in Lille. She had shown the letter to someone she thought was a friend and they had tipped off the police. Detectives raided Mrs. Spilers' house on 1 April and demanded the letter. It bore a Barcelona postmark.

'Darling,' Armand Spilers had written, 'I shall be on my way to South America by the time you get this. Don't think too badly of me. I am not such a villain as they say I am. I am in Barcelona now, but I shall leave as soon as I have written this letter. Here is some advice for you: those who seem to be always around you are not always your friends. Life is full of ambushes. I have good reason to know that. Live carefully. You are mine. I love you still, and one day we shall meet again when I am safely settled away from the hands of the police. Good-bye to you, my wife.'

Despite Spilers' warning his wife had shown the letter around and the police were on his track again. Spanish detectives raided the dives of Barcelona but, as Spilers had written, he had left the city after posting the letter. The only thing that could be said with certainty was that he had not been able to get a ship to South America.

Again he disappeared, but simultaneously a rash of daring burglaries occurred in south-west coastal towns in France. Police decided that Spilers had re-crossed the border and was collecting money to make his way to South America. But they could never catch him. It was not until early in September that he reappeared. Disturbed while burgling a shop in St. Jean de Luz, Spilers pulled a gun and shot down a fifty-eight-year-old policeman named Fatout. A police net went out and Spilers was caught.

Now he had a murder charge against him. He was put into a gaol at Bayonne under strong guard. But even then, on the night of 13 September, he managed to saw through the bars of the cell undetected. Knotting his blankets into a rope Spilers lowered himself silently from a second floor window, crossed a courtyard and scaled the prison wall. This time he was free for only ten hours before being picked up south of Biarritz heading for the border.

They took him back to Bayonne and shackled him to the floor of a cell.

Spilers was taken in an armoured car to the courthouse at Pau to face trial charged with a murder and sixteen robberies. Maximum security precautions were taken and Spilers was so heavily handcuffed, manacled and chained that he could hardly walk. They took him to the dock and six armed warders guarded him all the time. The prosecution had marshalled sixty witnesses against him. The defence had called upon a former guard from *le bagne* who testified that Spilers had been instrumental in saving the lives of three guards and thirty convicts when a boat overturned in high seas off St. Joseph.

The trial opened on 26 November to the popping of flashbulbs and a packed court. The following day it came to a dramatic stop when it was found that the foreman of the jury, Pierre d'Iriart, was not qualified to perform jury service. The judge ordered that Spilers be held until the next session of the court. He was taken to the prison and again shackled to the floor.

The second trial began as dramatically as the first. Again Spilers was taken into the courtroom in chains. The burglary charges had been dropped and so had most of the witnesses called for the first trial. This time the Public Prosecutor pressed the murder charge, demanding the death sentence.

'Spilers will get out of any prison,' he told the jury. 'That must not happen. He must pay the supreme penalty.'

On 5 February, 1937, only two days after the trial opened,

Spilers was sentenced to die. But the President of the Republic did not agree with the Pau prosecutor and on 15 May he reprieved Spilers from the guillotine, exchanging it for life imprisonment.

Now the authorities were thrown into a worse panic. Where could they keep the 'King of Escapers'? At midnight on 4 June a black saloon car with its windows blackened out pulled into the courtyard at Pau prison. Spilers, blindfolded, was hurried from his cell. He was being taken to another prison but the police had ordered that he must not know where he was.

It turned out that he was being returned to La Santé in Paris.

And then came a humorous touch in the Spilers' saga.

He was already doing a life sentence when, on 21 October, 1938, he was taken from La Santé to answer a charge of damaging Government property—one iron bar sawed in half in his escape from La Santé two years earlier.

Solemnly the judge sentenced Armand Spilers to ten months' extra imprisonment and back he went to La Santé.

Pierre Guillon had recovered from his knife wound and had made a precarious living as a prospector and as an orchid hunter. We got on well together and decided to team up.

I had a mad dream of going back to France after I had accumulated some money but Pierre Guillon said that it was crazy. His ambition was to get enough ready cash to go to Argentina and start a ranch. We did well during the two years that we worked in the gold camp. *Évadés* controlled everything there; the brothel, the stores and the selling of gold dust.

Early in 1947 Pierre suggested to me that we should go to Camaia, capital of the so-called 'Republic of the Desperadoes'. I agreed and we went down the river to Manaos and booked passages on a ship bound for Barranquilla in Colombia.

This incredible 'republic', officially recognised by both Venezuela and Colombia—in whose territory it lies—was founded about 1930 by a band of *évadés* who made an epic boat trip across the top of South America and managed to reach Colombia. They knew that a man could work and live on the coastal strip and it was their only hope. But they knew, too, that if they wanted to stay they must find somewhere that they could call their own.

In the interior of Colombia, Venezuela and British Guiana there are swift-running rivers where raw gold and rough diamonds can be panned and dug and huge stretches of jungle inhabited only by wild Indians. There are also vast, sprawling savannahs where a man can graze cattle or sheep and enjoy being free.

The fifteen convicts made their way into the interior by canoe and on foot and when they reached a point midway between the Orinoco and the Rio Negro they stopped. On that spot a small settlement grew up. They called it Camaia. It is not on any map. Soon more convicts joined them. Then two Americans came on the run from their own law. In time some Colombian bandits joined them and then some Venezuelans on the run from the Gomez regime.

One of the convicts journeyed to the coast to sell the rough diamonds and gold dust that the community had torn out of their new home.

It was a bold thing to do. He could have been arrested at once. And he could have just kept travelling, forgetting for ever about the men in the Camaia who were beginning to joke about their new home and were calling it the Republic of the Desperadoes. But he sold the gold and diamonds and bought some sheep for the community. They were transported up the river and across land where the feet of sheep had never been and they formed the nucleus of the flocks which graze today in the Republic.

The convicts made their own rules. They elected a president who had the power of life or death over his subjects. They elected a mayor to help him and a team of ministers. They made their own laws. For the first offence against a fellow Republican the penalty was banishment from Camaia for a specified time. For the second offence, a bullet.

At first the convicts raided isolated communities in Colombia and Venezuela. They carried off firearms and women mostly, for these were the two things they lacked. Sometimes they fought it out with the police patrols. A few died. So did a few policemen. Eventually the police learned to leave the convicts alone. These new men were hardened killers, not the rough and ready peasants-turned-bandits that the police were used to.

By 1944 the Colombian authorities, who had suffered most, were ready to recognise the Republic of the Desperadoes. A delegation travelled to the capital at Bogota and came to an agreement with the government. They would stop marauding and the government would stop molesting them. The Colombians had little use for the inhospitable and virtually inaccessible piece of land that the convicts called home. They were glad to be rid of the troublesome residents.

Since then Camaia has grown. The Republic covers an area nearly half the size of France. Of course it does not have officially recognised boundaries, but we who lived there know where it begins and where it ends. And Camaia, virtually the only settlement, certainly the only town, is in the centre of it.

Pierre Guillon and I travelled inland from Barranquilla to Camaia and spent about a week getting to know the place. They had a form of government there with rules of the camp, and people abided by them—for the most part, anyway.

We bought some shovels and pans and fitted ourselves out for an expedition into the foothills of the Andes where swift-running streams could be panned for gold and quiet little back-waters might even provide evidence of diamond deposits.

An American named Proud told us that he had just returned from an expedition which had yielded a good supply of small diamonds and had promised more. His partner had been killed by a snake and when Proud's food ran out he had had to return to Camaia for more supplies. He told us roughly where his strike had been made and said that he would see us up there in a few weeks. He also warned us that there were several small bands of convicts who were preying on others and said that a number of prospectors had been murdered in the area. The leader was an

American who had a knife scar across his forehead. One of his henchmen was German.

Pierre and I found where Proud had been working and moved farther up the river. We began sifting the gravel and found a few small stones. Things looked promising.

We had been there about a week when a man I remembered seeing at St. Laurent came into our camp. He had been working farther up the river but had been run off his diggings by some claim jumpers. One of them had a scar on his forehead. He said that his workings were about a day's trip up the river by canoe and he thought that the claim jumpers would work downriver and end up at Camaia.

Pierre and I talked it over and decided that we would keep very alert.

At dusk two nights later we heard voices and saw a canoe with three men in it passing down the river. One of them had a scar on his forehead. We thought that they had not seen us in our little backwater but then we heard them stop and the splash of paddles as they put ashore.

We built up our fire into a bright blaze and spread the blankets by it. There was only one way into the camp from the land, a narrow passage through the bushes.

I lay flat on the ledge straining my ears for the sound which would tell me that they were coming. My hand felt sticky on the butt of my .45 but I knew that when the time came I would know what to do. Over on my left I could hear the heavy breathing of Pierre. I wanted to tell him to breathe through his mouth but I was afraid to speak.

Then, suddenly, I saw them. They were coming down the little path which led to our camp. The moon shone for a moment on the rifle the first man was carrying. The path was too narrow for them to come abreast and they were walking Indian-style.

Pierre had seen them too. I heard a sharp intake of breath from him and hoped that he would not fire too soon. We had planned to let them get right into the clearing before we killed them. The last man had just stepped into the little clearing when I rose to my knees. They were uncertain for a moment. They must have expected to find us in the tent. Instead they saw what appeared to be two sleeping men, wrapped up in their blankets, beside the fire. They never had time to find out they were dummies.

My gun was bucking in my hand and I was screaming for Pierre to shoot. The first one went down as he opened fire. I saw the second one fall. Pierre had not panicked. The third man dropped his rifle and turned to flee. He got as far as the pathway and then a bullet from either Pierre's gun or mine smashed into his back. He fell and then scrambled to his feet. We both fired. He went down and this time he lay still. We climbed down from the ledge and approached the bodies slowly. My heart was pounding so fast I felt that I could hear it above the incredible din the monkeys and birds were making.

Pierre turned one of them over with his foot. It was the German. He had a neat hole above the right eye where the bullet went in, and the back of his head was torn away where it came out. The American with the scar had two slugs in his guts and was very dead indeed. The third man, the one who had tried to run, had two bullets in the small of his back and one in the back of his head. They had jumped the last claim they would ever jump. We dragged their bodies over near the fire and Pierre threw a tarpaulin over them. I put the coffee pot back on the fire and rummaged around in our plunder box until I found a bottle of white rum. We both had a good swig of it and Pierre lit his pipe.

The following morning I left him at the camp and paddled downriver to see the President of the Republic. We talked and I told him what had happened. I told him that other diggers had warned us that the men were claim jumpers and killers. That was all there was to it. The authorities had been informed and that was enough. I went back to our camp.

Pierre had already buried them at the back of the clearing and we carried on digging. Funny thing though. We never found another damned diamond there, though we dug for weeks. It had looked such a promising claim, but the first stones were also the last ones. Pierre said that it was some kind of retribution because we had taken the lives of three men. He was always superstitious—even though he had killed before himself. After all, they had come for us. It was kill or be killed.

I never knew how many people lived in the Republic, but Camaia has a population of ten thousand and there must be nearly as many again scattered about, ranching, digging diamonds or hunting. I wish I was there. I would have been, too, if I had not yearned to see France again. When I had made some money from mining I began to think about Central France and its lovely, rugged scenery. I talked to Pierre about it and he just laughed. He said that I would never be able to live there as a free man—and he was right. I thought about it a great deal, but never seriously intended to go back. It was just nice to think of home sometimes.

Then Pierre was killed. He was the only real friend I had. We had come to Camaia together and we were as close as brothers. Men like me do not make friends readily. And in the Republic, though there was little crime amongst us, a man had to know another one for a long time before he trusted him. There was always the feeling among us that the other man might be looking to rob or steal. As I say, there isn't much crime there. But there is some. Like the three men who tried to jump our claim. They got what was coming to them. The Republic was better without them.

We were mining diamonds in a remote river, just the two of us, Pierre and myself. We had dug a hole about six feet deep in the gravel and had then struck out at an angle making a tunnel as we went. We were shoring up the sides with boards from packing cases and it seemed safe enough. We worked it like this: one of us would crawl into the tunnel with a basket on a long piece of rope. That was left trailing behind. The one in the tunnel would fill the basket with gravel and then tug on the rope. The one standing in the hole would feel the tug and pull the basket backwards down the tunnel and begin to sift for diamonds. By the time he had sifted it the one who had been in the tunnel would have crawled backwards into the hole and the other one would go back up the tunnel with the basket. It worked well. We had a nice little poke of rough stones, better than we had before.

Pierre was in the tunnel with the basket that morning and he tugged on the rope. The tunnel was about forty feet long, give or take a few feet. I began to pull the basket back and had just got it into the hole when it happened. There was a rumbling and I heard Pierre's muffled voice yelling that the tunnel was caving in. It collapsed before he could get back. I grabbed a spade and began to shovel like a madman, but he was at the end of the tunnel and I had to shore it up again as I went. I hoped that he was trapped in a pocket of air and that I could reach him before he suffocated.

It took me more than three hours and the sweat was pouring off me in rivers. I was near exhaustion when I felt his feet in the darkness. I dug on frantically but he was dead when I cleared the gravel from on top of him. I dragged him back down the tunnel sobbing like a maniac. I buried the only friend I had in the world in that remote corner of the Republic and carved his name on a tree. I doubt if anyone will ever see his grave.

I went back to Camaia with a heavy heart. There is a trader who comes in twice a year to buy gold and diamonds that are dug up, and I sold mine to him for a good profit—if the loss of a friend could ever be paid for in money.

After that I began to have those dreams of France again and eventually I could bear it no longer. I went to the coast and bought a forged Colombian passport. Then I booked passage to France.

They arrested me three months later in Quimper. France was not like it used to be. I should have known that it would not be. I had not seen it for more than thirty years.

They had stopped sending men to French Guiana and the Salvation Army had repatriated most of those who were left there. They interceded on my behalf and said that if I had been in Guiana when they repatriated the others I would have been brought back. I had just 'come back under my own steam' was the way they put it.

I was let out of prison but told not to leave Paris. I have to report to the police every month.

It is a strange thing. In the Republic you are a virtual prisoner because there is every chance you will be arrested if you ever leave it. I was. Lots of others have been. But it is a big prison and there is always plenty to do.

I wish that I was back there now. Even without Pierre I would have made out somehow.

CHAPTER THIRTEEN

FRENCH COURTS SENT eighty thousand men to *le bagne* between 1852 and 1938, men from many lands, for many crimes. Frenchmen made up the largest group; then Arabs from the French territories in North Africa. After that came the Indo-Chinese, the Senegalese, the Malagasies and other French colonial subjects. Along with them were Germans from the border provinces and from the Foreign Legion, Spaniards from the border towns, Corsicans, Dutchmen, Belgians—even a handful of Britons.

The first—and most famous—British subject sent to Guiana was Eddie Guerin, born in Chicago in 1860. Guerin's father was an Irishman, from Limerick, who had emigrated to America in 1854 and died there twenty-one years later. His mother, a hard-bitten old woman, allowed petty criminals to use her home as a clearing house for stolen merchandise and young Eddie grew up among some of the toughest smalltime thieves in the windy city. He had already served several short terms in American gaols when he and Joe Butts blew the safe of the Pennsylvania Rail-road Company office in Pittsburgh and got away with $90,000 in 1882.

The pair fled to Cincinnati, Ohio, with their loot but Butts got drunk in a bar and talked to the wrong man. The following day both men were in the Alleghany County Prison. But the county gaol could not hold Eddie Guerin for long and soon he had made it over the wall and was on his way to New York and the big-city underworld. He found it harder to break into than the Chicago one and Guerin drifted around on the fringe for several months while trying to establish contacts which would get him into the inside of the criminal empire and eventually into the big money. But that was not to be. One night a raid on a down-town bar swept Guerin and sundry other lesser criminal lights into the hands of the police and he was soon back in Alleghany County Prison to finish his term for the Pittsburgh railroad job.

When he came out he became a 'bag man', operating switch jobs by duplicating bank messengers' bags full of currency for identical bags containing old newspaper. He liked to boast in later years that his most successful switch job netted him $63,000.

Money went through his hands like water through a collander and he went back to Chicago to spend what was left. The handsome young crook soon met a blonde who said she preferred him to her husband. Unfortunately for Guerin the husband was also a policeman and when he found his wife in a bar with Guerin one night he pulled his service revolver. Guerin was quicker and leaving the policeman with a bullet in his shoulder, he fled from the bar and took refuge in the underworld. He was advised that England would be a safe place until the heat cooled down. As a British subject Guerin could resist any attempts by the American Government to extradite him since Great Britain would hand over other nationals under extradition treaties but not her own.

Guerin reached London in time for Queen Victoria's Jubilee in 1887, picked enough pockets to set himself up for the time being and then went to France. In Paris he met Sophie Lyons, an American crook also on the dodge from the United States, who was masterminding a small gang of safebreakers.

On 2 July, 1888, with two other Americans, Bill Stetson and 'Dago Frank' Denin, Eddie Guerin blew a branch of the Credit Lyonnais, one of France's premier banks, got £8,000 and fled to London, reasoning that even if the French police did find out who it was they wanted, his British nationality would protect him from extradition.

Days later Scotland Yard picked Guerin off Bond Street at the request of the *Sûreté Nationale*. He appeared at Bow Street but the magistrate decided that he had not established his British nationality to the court's complete satisfaction and Guerin found himself back in France.

The French judge handed him a ten-year sentence at Rion, a tough and virtually escape-proof prison. Guerin spent all of the ten years trying to find a way out of the gaol but never made it.

It was 1900 when the French police released him and Eddie Guerin was forty. He was later to claim that he had been expelled from France as a British subject with a criminal record and therefore undesirable. Whether or not this was so he returned to London and then went back to Chicago.

But the city's police had long memories for men who carried guns—especially if they had shot an officer—and Guerin was soon tipped off that he had better leave. He picked pockets in New York, New Orleans, Cincinnati, and Pittsburgh—all his earlier haunts—before heading for Canada and then returning to London.

In a West End pub he met May Vivienne Churchill better known to her underworld associates as 'Chicago May', a blonde adventuress who, like his earlier friend Sophie Lyons, was on the run from the American police. Together they went to Paris where Guerin contacted two former associates, 'Dutch Gus' Mueller, a German, and Billy McManus, an American.

Together they blew the safe of the American Express Company on the Rue Scribe, collected $83,000 and split up.

When he thought it was safe to leave the city Guerin and 'Chicago May' went to a railway station and boarded the boat train for Calais. Unknown to them 'Dutch Gus' had been arrested with part of the money and had talked in the hope of making his sentence lighter. 'Chicago May' had left the train for a moment and Guerin was alone in the compartment when the police arrived.

He was tossed into La Santé prison pending trial and the first sight he got of 'Dutch Gus' was when they were brought into court—Guerin the accused and 'Dutch Gus', principal witness for the prosecution, the accuser. At the trial Guerin was surprised to learn that 'Chicago May' had been arrested in London and returned to France to receive a five-year sentence.

Guerin was given a life sentence in *le bagne* and later 'Dutch

Gus', for all his assistance to the police, was also handed down a life sentence. In December, 1902, they were taken to St. Martin-de-Ré to join three hundred Frenchmen also being transported on *La Loire*. The ship sailed to Algiers, picked up three hundred Arabs and Foreign Legion prisoners, and then crossed the Atlantic to Guiana.

Guerin had always lived well and the prospect of life in Guiana appalled him.

'There were times when the hopelessness of the future so completely took possession of me that I felt impelled to throw myself into the sea and allow the sharks to end it all,' he said later.

In June, 1903, Guerin was on Isle Royale when he formed a liaison with the young wife of the aging Commandant—so he lated claimed. Her attraction to the handsome prisoner led her to become Guerin's link with underworld contacts in the United States and she began to receive his letters bringing money for an escape bid. Guerin, as house-boy and gardener, made certain that the Commandant was satisfied with his work and when the official was transferred to St. Laurent he signed papers that authorised him to take Guerin along.

Once on the mainland Guerin knew his escape was only a matter of time.

He was put to work in the tailor shop which kept the warders' uniforms in good shape, manufactured suits for the convicts and *libérés*, and made canvas hammocks. Soon he found a kindred spirit in a Belgian named Julian Stoup who would join him in the escape bid. The Commandant's wife made the necessary outside contact through an Italian *libéré* who arranged for a canoe to be fitted out with a sail and provisions.

By February, 1905, Guerin and Stoup were ready. The Commandant's wife said a tearful good-bye to her lover and he promised to send for her as soon as he had gained his freedom.

But at the last moment 'Dutch Gus' discovered that Guerin was planning to leave and dealt himself in on the attempt by threatening to expose them if they did not take him along.

The three men crossed the Maroni and hid on the Dutch side

until dark. Then they put out to sea. They were still on the ocean six days later, harried by storms which blew them off course. On the eighth day 'Dutch Gus' went mad and flung himself into the water. The sharks got him immediately.

Thirteen days after leaving the Maroni, Guerin and Stoup staggered ashore near Paramaribo and were taken into the capital by Indians. There Stoup, who had a daughter living in Belgium, stowed away on a freighter hoping to get home. Guerin never heard of him again.

A local coaster took Guerin to Georgetown, British Guiana, and a few days later he stowed away on the *City of Quebec* sailing for America. He had a narrow squeak when the holds were searched at Martinique but he was not discovered and days later emerged, hungry and blinking in the harsh light, in New York.

Immediately he went back to Chicago and fell in with underworld contacts again. But soon his story was known and an alert newspaperman picked it up. Splashed across the papers the following day was the story of the man who had escaped from Devil's Island. By October, 1905, the French Ambassador in Washington had made an application for an extradition warrant and the Chicago police force were told to arrest Guerin on sight.

He followed his usual tactics of fleeing to Britain, again pinning his hopes on proving his British nationality if he were picked up by Scotland Yard. First he went to Leeds and worked as a tailor. Then he decided to settle in London. A few days after arriving Guerin ran into 'Chicago May', who had been released from the women's prison at Montpellier and deported from France. He never knew why, but 'Chicago May' sat down that night and wrote a letter to the police telling them that Edward Guerin, the notorious bank buster and escapee from French Guiana, had arrived in London. Guerin had given 'Chicago May' his address and she thoughtfully included it in the letter to Scotland Yard.

On a sunny April day in 1906 detectives picked Guerin off a Bloomsbury street and put him in Brixton prison pending further investigations and possible extradition to France.

Now Guerin had to work fast to avoid being sent back to *le bagne*. He wrote to newspapers as well as the Home Office and his case, of interest because of his unsuccessful attempt to prove nationality in 1888, and because of the more recent disclosures about Dreyfus and the conditions in Devil's Island, attracted a great deal of publicity.

When he came into court a year later to plead a case for refusing the extradition warrant, Guerin would have the best criminal lawyer in the business at the time.

But meanwhile, in Brixton prison, he had met a handsome Virginian just arrived from South Africa where he had specialised in burglary and petty larceny. His name was Cubine Jackson but he passed as Charles Smith and Robert Considine and he claimed, with complete truthfulness, that his Virginia family was one of the oldest and most respected and that through them he could claim kin to Lady Astor.

Guerin told Jackson of his troubles and of 'Chicago May's' letter to the police. Jackson commiserated with him. Lady Astor managed to get her relative released some time before Guerin was taken before the courts and unknown to the fugitive from *le bagne* Jackson and 'Chicago May' immediately teamed up.

On 15 June, 1907, Guerin appeared in the Divisional Court before Mr. Justice Darling and Mr. Justice A. T. Lawrence to plead his case. His defence counsel was Richard Muir, one of the country's top criminal lawyers.

The Crown's case was rested on the testimony of a Chicago policeman who claimed that he had known Guerin's parents in Chicago between 1860 and 1867 and who claimed that Eddie had been born in either 1860 or 1861. But Muir claimed that Eddie Guerin senior and his wife, the widow Fox, had travelled to Europe in 1860 leaving their son Patrick and widow Fox's two children by her former marriage behind in Chicago. They did not return to Chicago, until 1867 taking their new child Eddie Junior with them. His speech was so unusual that he was immediately nicknamed 'Cockney Guerin' by the locals. He had also lost two fingers from his right hand as a small child and

Muir produced an affidavit from the Chicago prison board that he had been unable to do recaning work on chairs while in their charge because of this. The policeman, MacMahon, said that the Guerin he knew had all his fingers.

Having thus thrown doubt into their Lordships' minds, Muir went on to read affidavits which showed that whenever the elder Guerin had been asked to vote while in Chicago he had always replied that he was a British subject and therefore not eligible to go to the polls.

He submitted that these affidavits were far stronger than the census record put forward by the Crown in the person of the Attorney General, Sir Lawson Walton.

Guerin's case was considered by the judges and Sir Lawson was forced to admit that, under the strong body of evidence, the Crown could not proceed with the case. Guerin was a free man.

As he stepped from the court he was mobbed by reporters. Later he was signed up by the *Weekly Dispatch* to write his story for them. The following day he was quoted as saying that the woman who had led him on the road to crime was in London, but said the paper, 'like a gallant Irishman, he peremptorily insisted that her name should not be disclosed.'

But Guerin had not seen the last of either 'Chicago May' or his former cellmate Cubine Jackson.

Two days after his British identity was established he was walking down Bernard Street on his way to his home when a hansom cab pulled into the kerb. As it drew to a stop a man leapt out of the cab firing a revolver at Guerin as he did so. The Devil's Islander turned to run, pursued by the man and a woman, the gun firing all the time. He fell at the third shot with a bullet in the foot.

By this time a crowd and a policeman had arrived and the man ran off, the constable closing on him rapidly. He turned and fired but missed the officer and, his gun empty, was quickly overpowered. The woman was caught as well.

Guerin was rushed to the Royal Free Hospital. The man and

woman were taken to the police station in Hunter Street and identified.

Days later Mr. Justice Darling, who had sat on the Guerin extradition case, was on the bench when Cubine Jackson, charged under the name of Charles Smith, appeared before him along with 'Chicago May' on an assault-to-kill charge. Charles Smith was sentenced to life imprisonment in Dartmoor and May to fifteen years in Holloway.

Guerin's story sold well in the papers and he became increasingly publicity conscious. He was too idle to work and used his Press clippings as a passport to a free meal and a drink with anyone who would listen to his story. When no one would, he lived by the only trade he knew—other than tailoring—theft.

In April, 1908, he was arrested for loitering with intent in the Bank of Montreal in London. In January, 1912, he was on the same charge concerning the Station Hotel, Glasgow. In May, 1913, he was arrested for drunkenness in London and a few days later was involved in an acid throwing incident with two prostitutes.

Then came the First World War and Guerin added to the war effort by working in a Midlands munitions factory. But by April 1918, he was back to his old tricks, being arrested for an attempted theft at the Metropole Hotel in Brighton. In September, 1920, he attacked a policeman in the Charing Cross Road when the officer tried to arrest him for loitering.

'Chicago May' was released from Holloway and deported in 1922 and soon afterwards Cubine Jackson, alias Charles Smith, was released from Dartmoor and also deported. In Chicago they teamed up again. He reverted to his other alias of Robert Considine and sold his memoires to newspapers as Guerin had done. But May was finished as a big-time criminal. When she died in 1929 she was penniless. Robert Considine just disappeared.

Meanwhile Guerin had been in more trouble. His long record built up and up: January, 1924, theft and assault in Edinburgh . . . May, 1928, loitering in the Regent Palace Hotel . . . November,

1929, theft of a suitcase on Victoria Station. In April, 1931, Guerin was back in the headlines charged with stealing a cheque book from the Strand Palace Hotel and forging the owner's signature. He was sent to prison, but successfully appealed on the grounds that with two fingers missing he could not have forged a cheque. After that it was back to the petty stuff: November, 1932, bag snatching in London . . . December, 1934, suspected person . . . May, 1935, suspected person in Jermyn Street . . . October, 1935, theft of eight pairs of socks in Regent Street . . . March, 1938, theft of a notecase in Liverpool—this time his victim was a detective . . . June, 1939, loitering on the Oaks course at Epsom . . . February, 1940, loitering with intent to commit a felony.

Between short prison sentences he either stole successfully or hustled for a living. And he collected his news clippings as soon as he came out of the prison.

Then came the Second World War. Guerin was at the end of the line. A broken, white-haired old man, he was put on a train at the height of the Battle of Britain along with hundreds of other refugees being evacuated to the country.

The journey ended at Bury, in Lancashire, and Guerin was put in an evacuees' home, persecuting his landlord with lurid tales from the past.

There was no one to mourn at his pauper's grave on 3 December, 1940, when he was laid away at the expense of the Bury Borough Council.

* * *

Soon after Guerin's escape another Englishman arrived in Guiana. He was V. St. Ledger Gould, who in 1879 had played in one of the very first tennis tournaments at Wimbledon.

In 1907 he murdered a girl in Monte Carlo and was sent to *le bagne* for life. He died there.

* * *

And there were others. Artists who had murdered their models in Paris; congenital thieves; deserters who had run foul of the French authorities; murderers from the back-streets of Montmartre. One who later published his story was George John Seaton, born in France to avoid the disgrace which his illegitimacy would bring upon his mother, whose family were connected with the peerage.[1]

* * *

In August, 1932, a ragged group of *évadés* staggered ashore at Siparia in the south of Trinidad. One of them was Marcel Maynard, an Englishman for all his French name. He had been serving a life sentence for killing his girl friend and had escaped nearly three months before in a sailing boat with five Frenchmen.

He told their story to the magistrates.

'We left Cayenne in May in a fifteen-foot boat with a small mast and sail. We had bought the boat for £12 which we had saved,' he told the court. 'Escape from the colony itself was easy. We were in the forest cutting wood and just walked away to the boat.

'When we had been at sea for about a month three of us became ill. We went ashore at Demerara (British Guiana), and the three of us were taken to a hospital at New Amsterdam, where we remained five weeks.

'The other prisoners went to Berbice, joined another fugitive expedition, and set sail for Trinidad.

'After leaving hospital we went back to our boat and set sail for Venezuela. While off the coast of Guiana we saw someone at sea signalling with a light. We went to the rescue and found four more fugitives sitting on an upturned boat. We took them on board our craft.

'For several weeks we wandered about, landing occasionally for food. One of our party died just before we were rescued by a passing British ship, the *Caribe*, commanded by Captain Percy Jackson. We were taken to Georgetown and placed in custody.

[1] See *Scars Are My Passport* by George John Seaton.

'Later we were given clothes and food and ordered to leave the colony.

'Again we set sail for Venezuela, but our boat was overturned four times by heavy seas and we had to land at Siparia for provisions.'

The Salvation Army took Maynard and his companions to their hostel in Port of Spain and eventually they were given a boat and asked to move on.

Where they went after that no one ever knew. Perhaps the ship overturned for a fifth time and drowned its occupants.

* * *

A year later another Englishman made a perilous flight across British Guiana. He and his companions reached Venezuela and were seized by the police. The French authorities immediately demanded their return and also the return of a woman who they said had financed the mass escape of her lover and twenty-one other prisoners.

Richard Henry Lucas, a sergeant in a Manchester Territorial Unit during the First World War, had two women in his life. One was Freda Jordan from Bakewell, Derbyshire, who served in the WAACs during the war and met him in France where they both saw service. The other was a lovely young French girl whom he married in Lille after the war had ended.

In 1924 Lucas returned to England to visit his family in Manchester and when he got back to Lille neighbours told him stories about his wife. She had been seen about with other men during his absence, they said. A few days later Lucas was on a murder charge, his wife having been discovered dead in bed with the marks of his hands round her throat.

At his trial Lucas pleaded not guilty of murder but guilty of manslaughter. He testified that he had gone to bed that night thinking about the stories he had heard about his wife's affairs while he was away. During the night, he said, he dreamed that he had found positive proof of her unfaithfulness and in the morning his wife was dead on the bed beside him.

His counsel put up a case that he had been disturbed in his mind and had strangled his wife while in the throes of a nightmare, but the judge rejected it and sentenced him to life imprisonment in Guiana.

The trial had attracted a great deal of attention and while he was awaiting transportation to the Ile de Ré to take ship for *le bagne* Freda Jordan returned to France and was granted permission to visit him. She promised to help him escape from the Settlements and start a new life in South America.

It took her seven years to save the money to reach Guiana and nearly three months to find out from *libérés* in which camp Lucas was held. In the spring of 1933 they were in contact and she began to lay plans. Eventually the night of 14 July was settled upon. It was Bastille Day and the guards would be celebrating in their club. The chances of running into a wandering official would be halved.

Lucas needed money for his break out, more money than either he or Freda Jordan owned. So he interested twenty-four other convicts in joining the escape and at an agreed time they left their huts and headed for a spot on the Maroni's bank a few miles below St. Laurent where an Indian was supposed to meet them with canoes.

In the dark they missed him and by morning a full-scale manhunt was underway with local trackers and dogs helping the guards in the search. It was the biggest mass breakout from St. Laurent up to that time. They could travel only in darkness and blundered about in the jungle for five nights looking for the guide. Snakes bit two of the men and they died. Another went mad and had to be killed because of the violence of his attacks on the others.

Eventually, on the sixth night, they contacted the guide who took them up-country to the hut of a *libéré* who could be trusted. The canoes had had to be sunk to prevent them falling into the hands of the guards who had combed the river bank looking for traces of the fugitives. On 30 July the 'fleet' was ready again and they put to sea slipping past the Galibi Light and heading westward for Dutch Guiana.

In the late afternoon of the first day they were spotted by a coastal patrol boat from St. Laurent but it was almost dusk and the darkness falls fast in the tropics. They slipped away into the night, but for a long time they could see the probing light of the patrol boat searching the sea for them.

The following morning sharks appeared and cruised perilously near to the dugouts all day. Near nightfall they saw land. They decided to put ashore and paddled towards a strip of sand on the beach. The sharks had apparently disappeared and when they were only two hundred yards off the shore four of the men jumped over the side and began to swim.

Immediately the dark fins cut through the water and before the swimmers could be dragged back into the dugouts the sharks had finished them.

The fugitives hugged the shore of Dutch Guiana all the following day and again decided to go ashore for the night. As they were nearing the shore Lucas slipped on the wet side of his dugout and fell into the water. A shark appeared, but he was luckier than the others had been and was dragged into another dugout just in time.

They landed in Venezuela and were well treated by the local fishermen. But the authorities gave them a choice. Move on or be sent back. They put to sea again. Several hours later another French patrol boat, far out of its territorial waters, sped towards them. They turned back and surrendered to the Venezuelans.

They were in need of medical treatment, suffering from exposure and too little food, so they were put in hospital pending a decision by the police and government.

British residents in the country petitioned on Lucas' behalf but eventually this was not needed. The authorities decided to let the men stay in Venezuela. The love of a woman for her man had sparked off the escape and the Latins are a sentimental people.

Richard Lucas and Freda Jordan moved south from Venezuela to make a new start.

*   *   *

It was a woman who got another former British soldier out of *le bagne* the same year.

James Harper, an NCO in the Royal Army Service Corps, was stationed at Rouen in 1915 when he met Madeleine Lenoir. They went out together for months and then had a quarrel. She moved away to Paris. A few weeks later Harper heard that she was living with a French flying instructor named Segrin. He issued himself a weekend pass and went to Paris to find them.

He forced his way into the house in which they were living and when Madeleine and Segrin returned from the cinema Harper was waiting for them with a gun. He shot Segrin dead and severely wounded Madeleine.

She was the principal witness against Harper when he appeared in court. The judge sentenced him to death for premeditated murder. President Poincaré later remitted the sentence to life imprisonment in French Guiana and Harper sailed for *le bagne* with the first batch of prisoners to go out after the war.

Most of Harper's time was spent in the 'bear pits' on St. Joseph. Altogether he made eight escape bids. On one occasion he sailed for British Guiana, hoping that he would be granted asylum in the colony. He was in sight of land—but still outside the territorial waters—when a French patrol boat overhauled his canoe and took him back to *le bagne*.

Meanwhile Madeleine Lenoir had decided to get him out of the colony. In 1928 she sailed for Brazil and made contact with *évadés* living in Belem. They were unable to find any trace of Harper—he was, at the time, doing a stretch in the 'bear pits' —and she used up nearly all her money trying to find out if he were still alive. She took a job to keep herself, deciding not to leave Brazil until she knew one way or another.

Early in 1933 a man arrived in Belem who had known Harper when he was on St. Joseph. He had been transferred to St.

Laurent, the man told Madeleine. And from St. Laurent escape was possible.

She went to Dutch Guiana and contacted some *libérés* who agreed to get a message to Harper in the St. Laurent camp. Then she bribed an Indian to pick him up at an arranged spot on the river bank and bring him across the Maroni to join her. They put out to sea and headed for Trinidad but were forced to land in Venezuela where the police captured them. British residents successfully petitioned the government not to send Harper back. President Gomez refused to honour the extradition request made by the French authorities.

* * *

Scotsman Hughie Watt was even more persistent in his escape bids. For him thirteen was not an unlucky number. After trying unsuccessfully to reach freedom on twelve occasions in fourteen years, he finally made it on the thirteenth attempt.

Watt, from Dumfries, was in Australia when the First World War broke out. The twenty-two-year-old immediately joined an Australian contingent and served in Gallipoli before seeing action in France. He was wounded four times and decorated for gallantry twice before finally being gaoled in the summer of 1918 for striking an officer. His decorations were immediately cancelled and while he was awaiting trial he broke out of the military stockade and headed for Paris. He was immediately posted as a deserter.

Watt made his way into the underworld of the French capital and assumed the name of Roger Guyot. Soon he was riding high on the crest of the post-war crime wave. In Montmartre he fell in love with a dancer and she threw over her gangster boy-friend for the man she knew as Guyot. A few days later the boy-friend and a companion, who belonged to a rival gang, cornered Guyot outside a café and pulled guns on him. But the Scots deserter was quicker than either of them and killed them on the pavement.

When he came before the court Watt thought it better to try an escape bid from *le bagne* than confess his real identity and be gaoled by the British authorities. So, in the name of Roger Guyot, he was sent to Guiana for life.

On two occasions after getting away from St. Laurent he was captured by Indians and returned to *le bagne* for the few francs the French authorities paid for *évadés*. On two other occasions he was caught by the warders and severely beaten before being sent to St. Joseph. Another time his dugout was overturned in heavy seas off the coast of French Guiana and he had to swim ashore where he was recaptured.

His thirteenth attempt came in January, 1937, when he got into the jungle ahead of some guards. He laid low for several days before making for the place where a canoe was hidden. When he eventually put to sea he reached Venezuela in a week, landing near the mouth of the Orinoco and surrendering to the authorities. Oddly enough this was one occasion when the French Guiana authorities did not press for extradition, being satisfied with Watt's explanation to the French Consul in Caracas that he was British. The Venezuelans, surprised by France's disinterest in Watt, allowed him to stay.

CHAPTER FOURTEEN

IMMEDIATELY AFTER THE war the Salvation Army began a campaign aimed at putting an end to *le bagne* for ever. The fighting had prevented any men being sent to Guiana after 1938 and the campaign began with pressure on the Government to allow the Salvation Army to repatriate all the *libérés* in the Settlements. Agreement was reached in 1946 and an old and defunct body, the *Comité de Patronage des Libérés à la Guyane*—set up in 1925 by the Minister for the Colonies—was re-constituted and activated. A sum of money was set aside and Captain Charles Pean was given a priority air warrant to fly to Guiana. He found great changes since his last visit.

'All the forest camps were empty,' he wrote. 'Charvin, the New Camps, Godebert, the Malagasies, were no longer in existence. At St. Jean, where two thousand men once lived, wild buffaloes grazed amid the abandoned buildings. Kourou was extinct. The Cayenne prison was empty. The Isles of Salvation had been evacuated. To date there remained only 837 *transportés* and 290 *relégués*, distributed between the camp and the hospital at St. Laurent, the tuberculosis camp and the lepers' island at St. Louis. The number of the *libérés* was about the same—1,059 in Cayenne, 857 in St. Laurent and 400 in other centres. In this number was included about 800 Arabs, 200 Indo-Chinese and 100 of other races.'

The rejuventated *Comité de Patronage des Libérés* undertook to get the men embarked at Cayenne. At the other end the Salvation Army was to receive the repatriates, lodge them and finally get them employed. The Arabs were to be sent directly to Casablanca, Oran and Algiers. European prisoners were to be sent in batches of fifty by the monthly mailboats, drawn in a ratio of two from Cayenne to one from St. Laurent. The Government guaranteed to underwrite three-quarters of the cost of passage, the repatriated convict one quarter. If he were destitute he was helped by the *Comité de Patronage*.

In August, 1946, the *Athos II* reaches Marseilles with 142 men, two orphan children of a *libéré* who had died on the eve of sailing, and two Guianese wives of *libérés*. In December the same year twenty-five men disembarked at Le Havre. In March, 1947, the *Colombie* docked at the same port with fifty-three *libérés*.

'*Le Bagne* is dying,' Captain Pean wrote in his diary with obvious satisfaction.

In April, 1947, a batch of Arabs arrived at Casablanca on board the *Boulogne-sur-Mer* and found Captain Pean waiting for them on the dock. One very old man who had spent most of his life in *le bagne* was helped down the gangplank by his friends. As his feet touched his native soil he smiled once and died.

'That was all he wished,' his friend told Pean. 'He wanted to die on the soil of Allah.'

The ship sailed on to Oran and then to Algiers where 200 *libérés* disembarked before she sailed on to Bone, the last port of call where the remaining *libérés* came ashore and finally split up. Some had to go to Constantine, some to Tunisia and then as far as the borders of the Sahara.

Another fifty-one men arrived at Le Havre in June along with the Salvation Army officers from St. Laurent. *Le bagne* was indeed dying and so was the need for a big Army staff in Guiana. On arrival at St. Lazare they were met by General Albert Orsborn, the Army's international leader. And so it went on: nineteen men in July—five of them Syrians and one from the prison colony at Noumea in the South Seas . . . eighteen in September . . . nineteen in October . . . twenty-five in December. René Boismoreau had been in *le bagne* for twenty years after killing his wife and his mother-in-law. One of his companions had been there thirty-five years.

But it was only the *libérés* who went free on their return. The *relégué individuels* were immediately interned in the Ile de Ré. Other who were too sick to travel had to remain in *le bagne*.

The repatriations went on. In January, 1948, another eighteen men arrived at Marseilles and seven at Le Havre; in February twenty-six more arrived; in April, twenty-four. The change in status of French Guiana from a Colony—under the Minister for the Colonies—to an Overseas Department of France—under the Minister of Justice—merely meant a change in the responsibility for the closing of *le bagne*. The Salvation Army went on as before, working in conjunction with the *Comité de Patronage*.

A voluntary journey from France to *le bagne* was made in early 1949 by Raymond Vaude, who had made a daring escape on 1 August, 1937, with three other convicts, one of them an Italian. After a 1,300-mile voyage lasting more than two months they paddled their twenty-five foot canoe into St. Thomas in the United States Virgin Islands.

'We crossed into Dutch Guiana where we obtained a canoe and left for Trinidad,' Vaude told the police. 'They forced us to leave and we drifted to St. Lucia where we stayed for thirteen days. Then we went to Dominica, Antigua, Tortola and then came on to St. Thomas.'

The Americans took the men to Puerto Rico and one of the Frenchmen and the Italian were detained there. Vaude and François Reau escaped to Haiti and Vaude returned to France at the outbreak of the war. He served his country as a saboteur and resistance agent blowing up German fortifications. After the war he called at the offices of the newspaper *Paris-Soir* and asked them to help him win his freedom. In February, 1949, he was granted 10,000 acres of land in French Guiana and left Paris to start a plantation in the land where he was once a prisoner.

During 1949 Salvation Army officers brought home 250 *libérés* on the *Ile de Noirmoutier* in January; another 250 arrived in May; and another 208 during 1950. The Army headquarters at Cayenne were closed at the same time and the officers sailed home.

Then the repatriation slowed. The Salvation Army needed a breather and statistics had to be compiled of the successful—or otherwise—repatriation of those who had already returned.

Their facts and figures revealed that of the 800 European

libérés repatriated before the war one had been sentenced to penal servitude for murder during the German Occupation; two others had received three-year sentences for theft; and two had received eighteen months for the same offence. Short sentences for petty crimes had been imposed on thirty-three men, sixteen of whom had broken the residence law. Of the total—thirty-eight—there were seventeen *transportés*, eighteen *relégués* and three military prisoners.

Numerous others had died. Some had done remarkably well. Pean reported that one was the chief accountant of a major business house; that another directed his own textile business in Lyons; and that a third had become the head of an industrial undertaking.

The convicts who had been brought back since the war had, for the most part, fitted in well. A few had been given short prison terms, mostly for breaking the residence law, which forbade them to live in big cities or in the same vicinity in which the crimes which had sent them to *le bagne* had been committed. One man had been illegally imprisoned for three months on the day he arrived in France.

Some, like Joseph le Borgne of Loudeac, could not fit in with post-war France. He had been sent to *le bagne* for poisoning his wife. When he came back there was nothing for him to do. He could not get adjusted and eventually he hanged himself.

He left a letter to his nephew in which he said: 'What am I doing back in France? I am only an animal which arouses the curiosity of everyone. Why? They say "No one ever comes back from there, but he has." My real punishment is here. The good life was in the colony.'

In June, 1951, repatriation was started again. The *Gascogne* brought eleven men home that month. In November the *Ile de Ré* brought twelve and two lots of five arrived in time for Christmas. September, 1952, saw the arrival of twelve men at Dieppe. A week later another dozen arrived. Two groups totalling twenty-four came the following month. On this last ship came seventy-eight-year-old Jacques Roussel who had served forty-five years for knifing a man to death.

The Salvation Army officer in charge of this mission in Guiana had travelled with this group as far as Martinique and then returned to *le bagne*.

'There are no more *libérés* to send home from here,' he cabled. 'The two groups which have left are the last of the men.'

A few weeks later he and his wife returned to France bringing with them the Salvation Army flag which had been taken to Guiana two decades before.

In 1954 another symbol of *le bagne* reached the end of the line. *La Martinière*, who had made her last voyage on 22 November, 1938, before going to Nantes to lie rusting in the harbour, was taken to St. Nazaire to be broken up for scrap. Newspapers hailed her as 'SS Black Maria' and justly called her 'the most terrible ship sailing the seas'.

In February, 1960, the French Finance Ministry, in an effort to raise nearly £52,000,000 to help with budget economies, put Devil's Island itself up for sale hoping that a tourist company might buy it and turn it into a rich people's playground. They offered a fortress, a hospital and forty cell blocks to any lucky buyer.

There were no takers.

Even in France there is still a sinister shadow cast across what was once *le bagne*. And there are still men in Guiana living out their lives as *libérés*—though this designation is now extinct. They are *relégués* who, having been denied residence in France, must remain in Guiana until they die. They are free men—but at the same time prisoners in the country, for they may never leave it.

Among them is the last of the old executioners of *le bagne*, a murderer named Mesnot, nicknamed 'The Fly'. He was the assistant to Leon La Durrell and took over from him. He could have been repatriated to France with the other convicts in 1947 but knew his life would not have been worth a candle. In Guiana while there were convicts there he had the protection of the guards. In France, with so many convicts free, he would have been on his own, at the mercy of the first man with a knife in his hand who could catch him in a dark alley.

He chose to stay in Guiana and will be there until he dies, shrivelled, despised, feared. He is a beggar in St. Laurent and people spit on him as he goes by.

CHAPTER FIFTEEN

ETIENNE ARTAUD IS a derelict little man today who scuffles for a living in the back streets of Paris.

He sleeps, when the police allow him to, in the gated entrances to the Metro stations. When they move him on, he picks up his bundle of old newspapers and his pathetically few possessions—a small wartime pack, a tin jug with a lid and a handle, a funny little bottle with a wired-on stopper—and moves on to try to find somewhere where they will let him get a night's rest. These things are all that he has now. These, his memories of a living hell in the French penal settlements the world knows as Devil's Island, and his memories of that strange and violent world in the Republic of the Desperadoes.

He is one of those who went back to France. Some have done well for themselves. Others fare little better than Etienne Artaud.

But *évadés* are scattered the length and breadth of the Americas. I have talked with them in ports in Central America, in the Caribbean islands and in British Guiana. They are to be found in almost every big city in South America. Some are respected businessmen. Some have risen to power in the wake of dictators. Others have run—and still do run—dope rings, white slaving gangs, dives, brothels and criminal syndicates. Some are merely tropical tramps.

One *évadé* now living in Port of Spain, Trinidad, told me: 'The Maroni boys don't usually bother to hide their identity if their new lives are legitimate. But if they are operating against the law they keep very quiet, of course.'

Another, now living in Nicaragua, told French writer François Poli: 'There are all sorts. Millionaires and paupers, respectable citizens and scum. I know some who own Cadillacs and factories, and others who are still prospecting for gold or tapping balata in the Brazilian forests eaten up with *pian* (a tropical disease which covers the body with blisters and sores) and sapped by fever. Then there are those who are kings of the white slave trade in Caracas and Rio, or who do drug-running between South and North America, and Europe.'

There were *évadés* in the Caribbean Legion, an organisation of professional soldiers of fortune which operated from a base in Central America, available as a private army to be bought by the highest bidder in the power politics struggles of the banana republics and South America.

A Corsican I met in Puerto Rico, where he was taking a holiday and living in style in a millionaire-class hotel, acts as a one-man military information service. Every time a revolution breaks out in Central America he knows who the leaders are, the strength of their armies, the number of their guns, the intriguers and plotters in the immediate theatre of war. This kind of information is readily saleable to any threatened regime.

There are probably some three hundred *évadés* scattered about the New World with an unwritten code binding them together, pledged to help each other if needs be—a sort of unofficial Freemasonry. The really successful *évadés* who have started new lives will help everyone—except the white slavers and the drug traffickers, whose taint could easily rub off if links were discovered, and totter any hard-won position.

'We aren't exactly a network,' one of these successful *évadés* told François Poli. 'Say rather a sort of family. We're bound to help each other. Anyone who comes from "up there" is like a distant relative, even when one doesn't know him. I don't mean the ones who are still in the drug or white slave business: we can't afford to have anything to do with them.'

'Up there' . . . '*la bas*', an unwritten bond between violent and desperate men.

* * *

René Belbenoit met many successful and prosperous *évadés* involved in crime while he was in Panama in the summer of 1931.

'Everywhere, in the coast cities between Argentina and Cristobal in the Canal Zone, and over on the Pacific side between Valparaiso and Panama City, these men made a good living from trafficking in white slavery,' he wrote later. 'There were thousands of Frenchwomen working for them, and, in addition, there were Polish women—and still others, who were being received into their hands in increasing numbers.'

Some *évadés* went back to Europe to act as agents for white slavers, setting up a network to send women to South America before the war. A few of them were captured. One was Roger Vernon who escaped from *le bagne* in 1927 and killed 'Max the Red' Kassel during a white slavery row in London's Soho nine years later. And in 1933 Paris police investigating white slaving got a lead on a man known as 'Dumas' who was staying in an hotel in a working-class part of the city. They discovered that he had already located two girls and sent them to Biarritz, promising to join them later. He was packing his bags when he was arrested.

The records of the *Sûreté Nationale* revealed that 'Dumas' was in fact Jacques Chevaller, who had been sent to Guiana in 1918 for communicating with the Germans during the First World War. They learned that he had served nine years before managing to escape across the Maroni into Dutch Guiana. He worked in wood and gold camps across Dutch and then British Guiana and had finally reached Venezuela where he managed to get a ship to Germany, hoping that his earlier contacts in this country would stand him in good stead. But his luck was out and he was deported. A stay in Switzerland ended the same way. And one in Belgium. Spain, using a forged passport, was his next stop and in Barcelona he joined a gang of white slavers who persuaded him to contact girls in France and get them across the Franco-Spanish frontier from Biarritz.

An *évadé* in Caracas has controlled a major part of the white slave traffic for nearly two decades. Another who travels frequently to Europe as a respected South American businessman has ten full-time agents working in European capitals for him.

When Antoine le Zouave died in Panama in April, 1931, he was worth over a million dollars. His son was studying medicine at an American university. Antoine's empire, built on white slavery, extended the length and breadth of Central and South America, across the Caribbean and into Europe.

In 1902 Antoine le Zouave was sent to *le bagne* to start twenty years hard labour for murder. A few weeks later he and twelve other *transportés* escaped in a canoe and reached Belem in Brazil. From there they took ship to Buenos Aires and Antoine borrowed money to send to France for his former mistress, a high-class prostitute. Her success in the Argentine capital was outstanding and soon Antoine was able to send for several of her friends. The *évadés* who had escaped with Antoine took over the girls as they arrived until each one had his woman on the streets. Buenos Aires became a meeting place for *évadés* and girls were lent to them until they got established and could send for their own.

In two years Antoine le Zouave was operating a big-time brothel with fifteen French girls working for him. His mistress had become the madame of the house which was patronised by high ranking officers, government officials, and, it was rumoured, the President himself.

Between 1904 and 1924 several thousand women were sent to Buenos Aires to be employed in the brothels of the *évadés*. Some came willingly as the contracted employees of white slaving contacts in France, Belgium, Spain and England. Others answered advertisements for 'secretaries' or 'showgirls' and arrived in the city penniless only to find that they were expected to work in the brothels. There was no one to turn to. Prevented from visiting their embassies by threats of violence and the vigilance of their employers, they were forced into the oldest profession in the world. Still others came with dance troupes and were lured into the big-time prostitution racket the same way.

Ten years after his escape from *le bagne* Antoine le Zouave owned ten houses of prostitution. His fellow convicts were nearly as prosperous. The trafficking in women increased and so did their wealth. It became so serious that in 1923 the League of Nations appointed a special committee to try to break down the white slave rings and four years later their statistics revealed that there were more than 6,000 French women living in the red light districts of every major port and city in South and Central America.

Argentina eventually closed down the large brothels and opened up a system of licensed houses of prostitution where each girl had her own room or *casita*. Antoine, now enormously rich and influential, obtained the exclusive right to operate the *casitas*. His profits rose to half a million pesos a year.

But eventually trouble of the *évadés'* own making caught up with them. They began to fight among themselves and shootings among their tight-knit community were common occurrences. The police, who had previously turned a blind eye and a greedy hand to the *évadés'* activities, now began to expel them. Antoine's influence and wealth stayed the hand of the law for some time, but then he too was told to leave the country. When he died a few years later after an appendicitis operation at the Gorgas Hospital in Panama he was worth well over a million dollars—every penny of it amassed from white slavery.

* * *

Other former inmates of French Guiana's prison settlements are smugglers in the Caribbean, some using light aircraft, some fast ships. They flit in and out of the tiny islands running perfume, rum, French wines and whisky. Often they spend days or weeks in French territory. One of the biggest smuggling centres in the entire Caribbean is the small French island of St. Barthélemy where their ships lie in the roadstead of Gustavson, untroubled by the authorities.

* * *

Some have risen high in the political regimes of Latin America or have benefited from political patronage.

When Cuba's dictator Fulgencio Batista fled before Fidel Castro's rebels one of his most trusted lieutenants went with him. He was Leon Garbet, who in 1927 was convicted of fraud in Marseilles and sent to *le bagne*. He was one of the first of the Maroni's former inmates to reach Cuba and when the little ex-sergeant Batista seized power in 1933 Leon Garbet went with him on the rise, becoming one of his confidential advisers and achieving great wealth and power.

* * *

Gilbert Pommier, sent to *le bagne* for burglary, became one of the richest men in Venezuela in the mid-'thirties and was one of the few not rounded up and sent back after President Gomez' decree that *évadés* be returned to French Guiana. In 1926 Pommier had crossed the Maroni on a raft and made his way right across Dutch Guiana and part of Venezuela to reach Caracas. Taking a job in a restaurant he became friendly with the proprietor and when the man wanted to sell out, Pommier bought the restaurant, paying by instalments. By now he was calling himself Pierre-René Deloffre and with the change of ownership of the restaurant—'La Suisse'—came a change of cuisine. Deloffre sent for his mother from France and 'La Suisse' became a French restaurant. Soon it was patronised by the cream of Venezuelan society. Deloffre married his cashier, hired more chefs and began to grow wealthy.

One night a diner confessed that he could not pay for the excellent meal he had just put away. Deloffre gave him credit then and on subsequent evenings.

It was one of the best moves he ever made. The diner was an ex-general, temporarily broke and out of favour with the Gomez regime. He and Deloffre became fast friends and when he got back into good grace with Gomez again the ex-general was able to pay off his debt and give Deloffre a few introductions which stood him in good stead. He was summoned to the Presidential Palace by Gomez and offered the post of Minister of Hotels and Entertainments, taking charge of Government-owned hotels throughout the country. It also meant that Deloffre, as a Minister, could exercise immense political power.

Few people at the top knew that the Minister of Hotels and Entertainments was an *évadé*. Certainly General Gomez had no idea. The impecunious diner whose influence had made the appointment possible knew and so did many of the ragged men who occasionally appeared in the streets of the capital. There is a certain something that marks a man from *le bagne* and which his fellows recognise immediately. Once Deloffre was faced with blackmail. He merely offered to empty his pistol into the blackmailer's stomach and that was the last he heard of the matter. Another time someone sent the French Consul a letter outlining in some detail the career of the burglar Gilbert Pommier—before and after his escape from *le bagne*. The consul sent for Deloffre and showed him the letter. General Gomez had not ordered *évadés* rounded up and deported at that time. Deloffre turned pale and felt sick, but the consul smiled and told him to keep the letter.

'It doesn't interest us,' he said mildly.

The same thing happened when a French journalist on a trip to South America found out the truth about the Minister for Hotels and Entertainments and published it in his paper. Deloffre, knowing that Gomez would find out, decided to tell the President before someone else did. Brandishing the paper he walked into the Presidential suite and showed it to the General.

Gomez laughed and said exactly what the French Consul had said: 'It doesn't interest us.'

Years later, long after the Gomez regime had ended—and the Minister of Hotel's job with it—Deloffre opened the Longchamp-Trocadero, a restaurant and club which was one of the top night-spots of Caracas. But then came a political upheaval which he could not ride. He liquidated what assets he could and fled to Brazil. Later he returned to Venezuela and bought a restaurant by the sea where he is said to be living still.

* * *

In February, 1962, a highly respected old man died on the Venezuelan island of Margarita which lies near Trinidad. His name was Dr. Pierre Bougrat and he was an *évadé*.

An officer of the Legion of Honour, handsome Pierre Bougrat, served his country as Chief of Hospitals during the First World War. His post-war practice as the leading skin specialist in Marseilles had been one of the most prosperous in the city. His name was one of the most respected in his profession. And then, on 30 March, 1927, he was convicted of the murder of his friend Jacques Rumebe and sentenced to life at hard labour in French Guiana.

Rumebe was a bank cashier. He had served with Bougrat during the war and the two men were close friends. Later, when Rumebe developed a skin complaint, Bougrat treated him free of charge. Then the cashier was found dead in Bougrat's surgery, his body concealed in a papered-over cupboard. At the trial Bougrat claimed that he had treated Rumebe for four years without ever asking or receiving a penny for his services and had used arseno-benzol in the treatment. Rumebe had died. He said that he had panicked, pushed the body into a cupboard and papered it over. Later he changed his story. This time he said that Rumebe had visited the surgery, confessed that he had embezzled money from his bank and spent it on high living. He then committed suicide and Bougrat, fearful lest he be implicated in the fraud, had hidden the body.

The prosecution's case was that Bougrat had known Rumebe was carrying £150 on him when he visited the surgery. They alleged that the doctor killed his friend for the money and then hid the body.

At one of the most sensational trials ever seen in Aix-en-Provence they sentenced Pierre Bougrat to life imprisonment in Guiana.

In *le bagne* a French Army surgeon and former comrade of Bougrat's, who was doing a two-year detachment as doctor at St. Laurent, applied for him to be made a medical assistant at the hospital. This was granted and for the first few months of his sentence Bougrat had an easier time than any of the seven hundred convicts who had been sent to Guiana with him. Then the St. Laurent doctor overheard talk in the Administration buildings that Bougrat was to be sent to the islands to be disciplined. He told Bougrat, handed him some money and advised him to get out if he could.

On 30 August, 1928, Bougrat and seven other lifers put to sea in a dugout they had bought from a Chinese merchant in St. Laurent. They set a course for Trinidad and for twenty-three days drifted at the mercy of the tides without a breath of wind to fill the flour-bag sail of the dugout. Storms lashed them and drove them off course. Their compass went overboard during a sudden squall that nearly capsized them.

Then the sea began to turn muddy and they knew that they were nearing the Orinoco delta—the Frenchman's Graveyard. The mudbanks that extended miles out to sea would trap a canoe and hold it fast. There was no way to free it. The mud was too soft to walk on and eventually the tides would turn the canoe over and the occupants would be drowned or sucked into the mud. The eight men were weak from the sea trip already. Any misadventure on the mudbanks would be the end. They decided to go ashore to recoup their strength and then make another try for Trinidad.

They landed on an island near San José de Amacuro, a small port at the southern edge of the Orinoco delta. But the people of the island were little better than the ragged, half-starved *évadés* themselves. Ravaged by plague, they hardly had the strength to bury the scores who died every day. There was no doctor—he had been one of the first to die.

Pierre Bougrat remembered the vows he had taken in France when he qualified as a doctor and set to work. Perhaps in the back of his mind was the hope that if he saved lives he might be spared by the Venezuelan authorities. It was true that *évadés* were not usually sent back from Venezuela at the time but they were often arrested as illegal immigrants and held while the French filed formal extradition papers.

Bougrat worked virtually night and day for the month that the plague was at its worst. At the end of that time he was beginning to see results. Fewer people were dying. Still fewer were going down with the disease. The supply of drugs left by the former doctor was almost depleted. But the epidemic had run its course.

Word of the saviour who had come out of the sea to rid the island of disease quickly spread. The police decided to investigate and on 28 October Pierre Bougrat and his seven *évadé* companions were arrested and taken to Caracas.

The Venezuelans refused to return the fugitives to *le bagne* and for a while Bougrat practised medicine in the capital. His companions took what jobs they could get. But two years later came the attempt on General Gomez's life by the *évadé* Sasse and the subsequent order that all French escaped prisoners be rounded up and returned to French Guiana.

To a man the islanders and mainlanders around San José de Amacuro petitioned Gomez on behalf of Pierre Bougrat. The President relented. The French doctor would be excluded from the deportation order. Gomez made only one condition: Bougrat could practise anywhere in Venezuela—except in Caracas. He could visit the capital—but he must not work there. Bougrat chose the island of Margarita as his new home. In time the Venezuelan Government recognised his talents as a surgeon and built him a modern clinic. He married an orphaned Italian girl and they raised three daughters. Life began again for the doctor.

But Pierre Bougrat had one weakness. He wanted to see France again. This he knew was impossible, but whenever a French ship was in La Guiara, the port for Caracas, he liked to visit the town and then go down to the docks to take a stroll. Usually he was invited on board the French ships to take a glass of wine with the captain, to smoke French tobacco and to speak his native tongue and hear news of his country. It was a poor substitute for the air and the feel of France, but it was better than nothing.

Then, on one of his visits to a French ship, the captain

decided to detain Bougrat and take him back to France and turn him over to the authorities. There would, he reasoned, be a reward for such an *évadé*. He locked Bougrat in a cabin and the cargo was loaded at speed. But Bougrat managed to get word to a dockhand he knew and the man told the Venezuelan police. President Gomez was informed. He sent an order to bar the entrance to the harbour and then sent a police inspector to see the French captain.

'Release Bougrat or your ship will not be allowed to sail,' the man was told.

After that incident Bougrat gave up visiting La Guiara. He grew very wealthy and built a magnificent home on the island of Margarita and his daughters grew up there.

In the twilight of his years Bougrat hired an expensive firm of Venezuelan lawyers to try to persuade the French authorities to allow him to return home for a visit. *Le bagne* had been closed and most of the convicts had been returned to France. There seemed to be no reason for Bougrat's request to be refused.

But a vengeful French Government turned him down. Bougrat was an *évadé*. He had broken the laws of France by killing a man. He had broken the laws of *le bagne* by escaping.

The petition came back marked: 'Rejected'.

In 1962 Pierre Bougrat died in his villa overlooking the Caribbean. He was seventy-two. He had just one regret. He had not died on French soil.

To the Venezuelans he was a hero; to the French a wanted man.

* * *

Lucien Gardot, blackmailer, paid his personal debt to society by escaping from *le bagne* and going to work in a leper colony off the South American coast.

* * *

The head of one of South America's most important metallurgical works is an *évadé* who, complete with Spanish name and locally issued passport, lives respected and undetected. Another man went to the United States, became a naturalised citizen, eventually bought two clubs in Las Vegas, sold them and today runs a popular night club on the Pacific coast. Yet another escaped from French Guiana and made a fortune as a coffee planter in Costa Rica before retiring to a luxury villa near Fort Everglades, Florida.

* * *

There are, too, the convict empires in Brazil and in the Venezuela-Colombia border country. Today there is a gold rush up the Amazon and *évadés* were among the first to arrive with shovels and pans. But the indications are that Venezuela and Colombia are soon to make a move against the men of Camaia—capital of the 'Republic of the Desperadoes'.

And then where will the last of the damned call home?